Learning from Work and Community Experience: Six International Models

Contributions by
Per Dalin, Bruce Dollar, Val Rust,
Leendert van den Bosch, Noel Kershaw
and Magne Skrindo

Edited by Heather Chisnall on behalf of IMTEC
(International Movements Towards
Educational Change)

NFER – NELSON

Published by the NFER-NELSON Publishing Company Ltd.,
Darville House, 2 Oxford Road East,
Windsor, Berks, SL4 1DF

First published 1983
© International Movements Towards Educational Change, 1983.
ISBN 0-7005-0620-9
Code 8153 02 1

Photoset in Plantin by The Eastern Press
Printed in Great Britain

Distributed in the USA by Humanities Press Inc.,
Atlantic Highlands, New Jersey 07716 USA.

010821173

Contents

Preface

IMTEC

IMTEC (International Movements Towards Educational Change) – The International Learning Co-operative is a Norwegian-based foundation committed to the study of change and innovation. The volume *Learning from Work and Community Experience* is the result of cooperation among a small group of practitioners in North America and Europe who have studied the concept of participatory learning – the idea that an individual can learn in a non-formal setting through participating in a work or work-related experience normally outside the framework of the school system – and who, through IMTEC, has undertaken a series of cross-national field visits. In the course of these visits, we discovered more and more about the vast field which is 'Learning by Participation', and we find we are in no way finished with the work.

The Term 'Learning by Participation'

The term 'Learning by Participation' is a simple and convenient way of referring to the concept given above, being sufficiently close to existing terms in Scandinavia and The Netherlands to be meaningful across national boundaries. It has been employed throughout this book.

Networking

IMTEC will continue to disseminate information about Learning By Participation. An informal network of practitioners and researchers has already been formed, which network any interested person might join. We shall continue to organize field studies, provide information about projects and to bring people together for international discussions. We see these as important activities in a new field like Learning by Participation. We also hope that organizations such as UNESCO, the European Community and OECD will put more emphasis on Learning by Participation developments.

Research

We know little about the impact of participatory learning programmes. Therefore we hope to attract foundations to fund research projects that will help us to learn about it. We consider, for example, that it would be very useful to compare programmes in a more vigorous way across cultures. Further conceptualization in the field is also necessary. Most important, maybe, is to create a forum for researchers in the field which will help them support each other in their work – in the field of programme evaluation in particular most countries have limited experience. Models and designs could usefully be exchanged, discussed and applied.

Development

Most importantly, Learning by Participation is a creative activity in which the central creative force is the individual teacher and her students. We see great potential in bringing teachers and students across cultures into contact with each other to exchange experiences, programme ideas and materials. That would certainly be learning by participation in its own right.

The Book

With regard to the book itself, we make several cautionary observations.

First, even though the authors have collaborated closely with each other throughout the writing, they have been confronted with the dilemma faced by any who attempt in-depth comparative analysis. Strictly, comparative studies require a level of abstraction in terms of categories, problem statements, and processes to the point where findings inevitably lose some touch with social reality. However, if the authors had avoided abstractions entirely and had remained locked too firmly into their cultural situations, no generalizations at all would have been possible. In this study we have chosen to take a middle ground in that we have relied upon a common conceptual base and have dealt with parallel problems in each chapter. However, the various authors have been allowed the freedom to discuss their own situations within the frame of reference of their respective national contexts (it must be remembered that Learning by Participation is a concept, not a programme, and as such takes different forms in different countries according to the differing circumstances in each).

Consequently, any generalizations that have been used must be considered to be very tentative. Such a limitation has little to do with the competence of the authors or with thoroughness of treatment, but addresses itself to the dilemma inherent within cross-cultural analysis.

Our second cautionary comment is that we shall avoid making judgements about the relative value of specific programmes. Very few of the projects discussed in this book have been subjected to rigorous evaluation, and we are in no position to assess their relative quality even within the cultural context where they have been organized.

Thirdly, we should like to warn the reader against the tendency towards attempting to transfer experiences from one culture to another. We believe that it is possible to learn from a Learning by Participation project in another cultural setting, but we do not believe that experiences are easily transferable. Each local system needs to find its own solutions. That is, it needs to undergo its own process of self-assessment, adaptation of programmes exisiting elsewhere, and creation of new programmes. Although we consider this volume to be important, it can only serve as one of several impulses that might trigger off an innovation process within a local system.

Per Dalin
Director, IMTEC

CHAPTER ONE
Learning by Participation

BRUCE DOLLAR and VAL RUST

Introduction

The universal concern for the way in which young people are prepared for adult life has given rise in recent years to a world-wide interest in learning opportunities for youth based on their active participation in society. This interest has been kindled by a growing awareness that traditional schools tend to isolate children from society, channel their learning in narrow academic ways, and cut them off from much valuable real-life experience. Accordingly, in countries throughout the world, a wide variety of programmes has appeared which break down the artificial barriers between school and community and give young people important roles to play in the adult world.

In Skedsmo, Norway, fully one half of the lower-secondary pupils of participating schools have elected to spend Monday and Friday of every week learning in the industrial, commercial, or service sector of their community. In India, young join with old to participate in nationally-sponsored community development programmes aimed at improving agricultural productivity, roads, health, and sanitation as well as more formal education programmes. In the United Kingdom, students at Garth College have worked for years on a long-range programme to transform an old Victorian garden into a public open space including a greenhouse, a Japanese garden, and an open-air theatre. In Cuba, young secondary school students migrate into the countryside for extended periods of time to help the rural population overcome its general educational and literacy weaknesses. In Canada, a 16-year-old student voluntarily devotes 10 hours a week in a social service capacity, where she develops skills and a commitment to solving local social problems. All of these examples have one thing in common. Young people are learning by direct participation in the life of their community.

We have chosen to describe this type of education as Learning by Participation (LBP), an approach to formal education that aims at meeting the developmental needs of young people by linking learning gained by taking meaningful roles in society with the study and reflection that are associated with conventional education programmes. Through LBP school learning is no longer separated from the broader society, and young people assume responsibilities that help them develop abilities to function as mature and productive adults. LBP provides opportunities for the young to learn by taking part in the real social world. It encourages cognitive learning, concept formation, and abstract reasoning mainly as these relate to action and experience in the present world.

The authors of this book have three major objectives. The first is to explain Learning by Participation by placing it in its socio-historical context and by providing a conceptual framework for further discussion. The second is to describe the form and the content of actual LBP programmes that are being implemented in a variety of national settings in Scandinavia, the Netherlands, the United Kingdom, and the United States. The third objective is to consider key issues related to the implementation of LBP in these and in other countries.

Although we expect it to be of great interest to the student and scholar, as well as to the informed public, the book is primarily directed at the educators: decision makers, teachers, and other practitioners. Our intent is to open a dialogue among these people that will contribute to greater understanding, better practice, and wider acceptance of Learning by Participation. We also hope that our efforts will result in the emergence of an international network of people who share an interest in LBP, and who will provide the impetus and the critical mass necessary for it to become more widespread than it is at present.

We have restricted our treatment of LBP in this book in two arbitrary ways. First, we have focused our attention on the Western industrialized nations in general and the four geographic areas mentioned above in particular. The choice of these areas can be explained on simple, pragmatic grounds. Although programmes incorporating learning by participation are being developed in other countries, we are most familiar with those in the areas we cover here. We have found these to be sufficiently diverse and exemplary to illuminate most of the issues involved in LBP-related programmes in comparable Western countries. Furthermore, collaboration in cross-national exchange and development programmes based on LBP has already occurred among these areas. This has given the authors, who have been personally involved in these activities, an opportunity to arrive at a common conceptualization of LBP that insures a harmony and continuity not possible in most international multi-authored works.

Second, we have chosen to concentrate our discussion of LBP on programmes for adolescents or young people. We do not attempt a specific definition of this age group, which occupies roughly the period between 'dependent childhood' and 'independent adulthood' (two arguable and somewhat presumptuous terms in their own right, which we shall not venture to defend). The schooling of adolescents is typically at the secondary level, but this, too, cannot be strictly defined in an international context. By no means do we imply by our choice of focus tht LBP is not appropriate for other levels of education. We insist, in fact, that it is vital to learning and growth for the very young as well as for the mature adult. But the problems suffered by adolescents in the present world seem especially urgent, brought on, we feel, by a failure of the policies and institutions that ostensibly serve youth to have adjusted to important changes in the societal context of young people that have accompanied modernization. It is precisely this failure that Learning by Participation is designed to remedy.

This chapter provides an introduction to the general concept of Learning by Participation, and, thus, to the more specific country-based chapters that follow. After describing the present needs of both youth and society to which LBP is addressed, we briefly trace the historical development of schooling from its narrow and specialized role in pre-modern Europe and North America to its incarnation in present-day industrialized society as a mass institution with pervasive social and economic effects. Following this are brief case descriptions of two typical young individuals in two different countries that illustrate the impact of these conditions on the lives of young people. Finally, we propose a working definition and a conceptual framework for Learning by Participation which are explained and illustrated using examples from actual LBP programmes in various countries.

The advent of post-industrial society has brought significant changes in patterns of youth development. The central roles once played by such social institutions as family, religion, and neighbourhood in lending stability, continuity, and community integration to life have been greatly altered or diminished, while the school and the peer group, almost by default, have taken on commensurately larger significance as major socializing influences in the lives of young people. Unfortunately, these new patterns have left broad areas of needs substantially unmet. Both the schools and the peer-group subculture tend, for different reasons, to isolate young people from experiences that are vital to healthy development. At an age when identity and self-worth are primary concerns of young people, they are given no useful role in society, and few opportunities to demonstrate their value as human beings. Schools require students to remain passive in learning, and dependent on adult authority and bureaucratic structure. Not only does this stifle their need for action and their willingness to learn, but also it leaves them woefully ill-equipped to cope with society as independent, responsible adults. Their sense that society has no significant role for them where their presence makes a difference leads most adolescents to rely on their own peer group to supply action and a place to belong.

Adolescents in modern cultures occupy a void in the social structure. No longer children, but not yet adults, they are considered transitional beings who must spend their time – the period of 'vestibule adolescence,' as psychologist Kenneth Clark has called it – in preparation for eventual adulthood. Rather than allowing this preparation to grow out of and be the product of present activity, however, preparation has come to be equated with postponement – with the acquisition of concepts, skills, and information to be applied at some future time. Accordingly, adolescence itself has come to be equated with waiting. As one contemporary text puts it, 'adolescence, then, can be defined as a *holding period* in which education, maturation, and waiting are the major tasks to be faced.' In his essay *Experience and Education*,[1] John Dewey explored this misconception of preparation:

> The idea of using the present simply to get ready for the future contradicts itself. It omits, and even shuts out, the very conditions by which a person can be prepared for his future. We always live at the time we live and not at some other time, and only by extracting at each present time the full meaning of each

present experience are we prepared for doing the same thing in the future. This is the only preparation which in the long run amounts to anything.

The concept of adolescence as a waiting period reflects society's failure to understand or respond to the needs of young people. Policies toward youth in most of the Western industrialized countries fail to see that many of the 'problems' associated with contemporary youth are the direct result of conditions that consign them to social and economic limbo. Instead, those policies seem based on a 'social deficit theory' which, mistaking symptoms for causes, aims primarily at correcting shortcomings in the youth themselves. Thus, youth 'alienation' is ascribed to loss of self-esteem and other psychological factors; rebelliousness is explained as a 'normal' adolescent pathology; and counsellors are assigned to help troubled young people to cope with these 'personal problems.' Similarly, youth employment is attacked by training progammes, as if the problem lay in the competence of youth rather than in discriminatory laws and practices or in the sheer absence of jobs. In the United States, such approaches to solving social problems are called 'blame the victim' policies.

How did we reach this state of affairs? Why are institutions ostensibly designed to serve youth so out of line with their needs? Why does public policy seem so incapable of recognizing its own shortcomings? How did schools become so divorced from society, and why do they seem to have reneged on their promise to equalize economic opportunity? The truth is that modernization has changed both the social context of youth and the role of schools. These changes must be understood if one is to appreciate the plight of contemporary youth fully. The necessarily brief historical analysis that follows attempts to shed light on these changes by focusing on the changing social and educational role of schools.

The Evolution of Modern Schooling

During the modern age, a distinct ideological trend may be traced with regard to the relative influence of in-school and out-of-school learning. Modernity is marked by an increasing tendency to establish the school as the certifying educational institution (Rust, 1977).[2] During the past two centuries, modern nation states have systematically sought to rid themselves of diffused traditional learning practices and incorporate these into formal schooling programmes.

In pre-modern or traditional Europe and North America, educational environments were primarily non-formal and informal. That is, education was largely the responsibility of institutions which did not define their main task as being educational. The household, the church, and economic institutions such as the guilds, simply assumed that they must educate, and they incorporated systematic educational programmes into their activities.

Traditional education was also largely experiential in that it was conducted as a part of the on-going affairs of life. For example, for several hundred years prior to the establishment of the modern industrial state, apprenticeship was the major formalized mechanism to prepare the young for special crafts and trades. A child was entrusted to a master, who was obligated to care for his needs from his sixth to his sixteenth year. The youth was inducted not only into the skills of the craft, but the total life-style of the master. In the process he gained a general education, of context and history, not so much in terms of information but in the customs and beliefs of the guild and its role in the community (Abraham, 1957).[3] Very little of this learning took place in a school-like setting.

Schools did exist in traditional societies, but their importance to the general populace was limited, and those few scholars who participated in extended schooling prepared themselves thereby to engage mainly in such professions as the church, medicine, and the law.

The general pattern of schooling throughout traditional Europe was remarkably uniform consisting of content-mastery of books and lectures by the student interspersed with standard disputations and debates about their content. Even medicine was treated deductively, and masters did not consider direct experience of observation necessary because it only contaminated their systems of thought.

With the advent of the modern age, school became the educational ideal for almost all forms of learning. This ideal was never fully realized, in that vestiges of traditional experiential practices continued in certain forms, but the general value-orientation toward schooling was clear. The grammar schools and universities, while altering their major purposes from the training of scribes and religious leaders to leaders of state, nevertheless retained their traditional orientation toward a classroom instructional process. Mass schooling, while altering its aim from an exclusive devotion to the church to include devotion to the nation state, also perpetuated a classroom instructional mode. Consequently, for the first time in history, the modern age set the ideal that all youth would benefit from an extended schooling experience.

While the major early modern motives for mass schooling were largely religious and political, these were soon overshadowed by the budding demands of the industrial states of Europe and North America. Industry came to provide even the structural model for mass schooling in modern countries. Schools were organized like the conventional modern factory. Teachers and other personnel as well as their tasks were differentiated into ever smaller and simpler cells, which were in turn integrated again to process the raw material of society. School programmes were divided into grades, subjects of study, talent tracks, and sections. Recent analysts now recognize that 'the whole idea of assembling masses of students (raw material) to be processed by teachers (workers) in a centrally located school (factory) was a stroke of industrial genius' (Toffler, 1970, p. 400).[4] The very structure of the school and the processes which took place within that structure prepared the youth of the modern world to function according to industrial imperatives. Children marched from station to station and bells rang to signal when to change work stations. Discipline and habits of punctuality and precision and respect for authority were imparted in such a manner as to insure industrial productivity. School administration also came to model industrial management as the 'cult of professionalism,' which with its focus on efficiency and speed, further solidified the industrial model of schooling.

Paradoxically, while the school modelled itself after the modern factory, the actual instructional practices of the individual classroom remained very traditional, with the media of instruction remaining as the teacher and the book. On the one hand, children learned in the school how to function in modern industrial institutions, while on the other hand, the actual curricular packages were transmitted either through a verbal or a written medium, both being highly symbolic in nature.

The impact of these developments in schooling on the participation of youth in learning should be obvious. As the school age and the number of attendance days each year were extended, the time available for participation in other modes of learning was reduced. Apprenticeship in industry, agriculture, and business was all but swallowed up in certain Western countries, to be replaced by schools. Homemaking was no longer learned in the home but in the school. Even recreation and physical exercise became compulsory school subjects.

It was the latter part of the nineteenth century before the schools began to pay attention to learning methods other than those found in traditional schooling. With the advent of teacher education programmes using the pedagogical ideas of such men as Pestalozzi and Herbart, more concrete forms of learning began to appear in classrooms. Teachers became committed to the development of school museums where artifacts and specimens could be used in 'object lessons.' Wall maps, globes, solar demonstration kits, balls and cubes became common in the classroom, and science laboratories began making their way into the schools. The 'natural' method of language instruction slowly began to challenge the traditional 'translation' method, and teachers began to lay stress on oral competence and acquaintance with foreign *mores* and customs.

With these modes of instruction, modern education moved into a new phase with regard to experiential learning. Although learning remained largely school-based, there was increasing stress on actual doing as a part of learning. Most of this was still restricted to simulations of direct practices through well-designed laboratory exercises, using industrial arts equipment, and even through cooking and sewing classes. In the United States, the fullest expression of this orientation of modern education came with the work of John Dewey, who founded a laboratory school at the University of Chicago specifically intended to develop a schooling model that would fulfil a more appropriate educational role for schools in the modern age.

Dewey believed that the modern child lives in a world of manufactured products and yet is separated from the processes through which these products came into being. In contrast, in the pre-modern world 'the entire industrial process stood revealed, from the production in the form of the raw materials, till the finished article is put to use' (Dewey, 1970, p. 10).[5] Children in this earlier society came to understand the means through which society survived and flourished as a matter of course. Modern society had destroyed this integrative force, and Dewey defined the new task of schooling as one to help children to reintegrate the social, economic, and political processes which their everyday environment could no longer teach them.

Dewey's laboratory school was intended to recreate an embryonic working model of the larger industrial society. The school environment consisted of learning centres in which the child could become familiar with woodwork, tools, cooking, and textiles. We see in Dewey the embodiment of the experiential model of Progressive Education and the New Education of Europe. The school was to cease being exclusively abstract and symbolic; through experience-oriented education it would give young people a sense of identity and an understanding of their broader community.

Experience, however, was mainly, though certainly not exclusively, restricted to a simulation of the real conditions which the progressive educators perceived to be the cornerstones of the contemporary world. For Dewey, the school was intended to swell beyond its walls and 'secure an organic connection with social life' (Dewey, 1970, p. 79),[6] but its main energies were directed internally, toward the social life of the school itself. Even Dewey's school was intended to shield children from the outside world.

Dewey was but one of several outstanding spokesmen for reform after the turn of the century. Blonskij in Russia, Kerschensteiner in Germany, Freinet in France, Decroly in Belgium, each expounded his own unique version of reform. Following the First World War, these forces jelled into a movement with a common identity which flourished through the 1920s and 1930s. In the 1940s, a moratorium was called on progressivism and the New Education while European and North American nations got down to the business of war. Following the war, these movements never fully recovered their impetus. However, their impact on schooling at large was significant, as excursions, field trips, individual and group projects inside and outside the school, as well as visitors to schools from various walks of life, tended to help education maintain a thread of contact between the school and real life (Cremin, 1964, p. 349).[7]

However, before contacts between the school and social life expanded beyond the nominal links just mentioned, the schools of Europe and North America retreated significantly back to school-oriented reform. The 1950s and early 1960s have often been characterized as the period of innovation and change; Charles Silberman characterized United States efforts as 'one of the largest and most sustained educational reform movements in American history' (1970, p. 153).[8] However, these efforts never attempted to link schooling with broader social life, perhaps because of their point of origin. Goodlad points out that 'they were conceived primarily by scholars in colleges and universities who were joined by teachers from elementary and secondary schools' (1964, p. 10).[9] Consequently, they focused on curriculum design, classroom instruction, teaching technology, and various staffing arrangements, all of which were internal 'schooling' adjustments. Inquiry consisted, at times, of simulation exercises, but neglected learning tasks connected with real life almost completely.

Contemporary Critiques of Schooling

In the late 1960s, a time of social upheaval in many of the industrialized countries, the schools suddenly came under sharp attack for the role they had come to serve. As the tide of protest against schooling developed, the thread of contact which progressivism had created between school and real life was hardly sufficient to quell the claims of the irrelevancy and discontinuity of schooling with the broader social reality. Other discontents stemming from economic, social, and political factors were soon added to the criticisms against schooling. The critics took note, as we have, of the role of modernization in producing an increasingly technological, urbanized, and mobile society, which heaped new demands on the school.

Formal schooling had come to be viewed not only as the most reliable means of imparting the skills and knowledge required by a rapidly changing industrialized world, but also as a means for greater numbers of young people to gain a foothold in the labour market. The ideal of mass education seemed to promise to all what had previously been a privilege of the elite. However, the concurrent decline of the traditional socializing institutions for the young – including work, family, religion, and community – correspondingly placed that burden on the schools. The schools had been vested with the primary responsibility for socializing the young for adulthood, a task for which they were only partially equipped.

School critics of the 1960s also called attention to a radical shift in the relationship of schools to the economy; where once schools had provided young workers for the labour market, now they served to keep them off. The decline in unskilled jobs and the need for greater skills that came with industrialization made it necessary for young people to postpone their entry into the work-force. One aspect of the schools' expanded role was thus to occupy the young until they could be absorbed as workers. The period of formal schooling was accordingly prolonged through adolescence and into early adulthood.

Unfortunately, the critics pointed out, the organization of the schools as mass institutions directly conflicted with their purported role as teaching and learning institutions. In keeping with the contemporary values of the industrial and bureaucratic state, the mass school was modelled to maximize efficiency and control. With a structure constisting of age-specific groupings of students, graded and sequential curricula, and teacher-classroom production units, the schools came to mimic the rituals of the factory, stressing the virtues of obedience, silence, punctuality, and acquiescence. Theoretically organized to transmit knowledge, the schools were more accurately described as mass custodial institutions that effectively isolated the young from the adult world. Attempts to soften or 'humanize' the schools by reformers dating back to John Dewey (1916)[10] and A.S. Neill (1969)[11] did not alter the predominant fact of school life: students were kept in a state of utter passivity and dependence.

By the early 1970s one branch of criticism had coalesced around the provocative notion of 'deschooling society,' a phrase coined by Ivan Illich (1971).[12] The deschoolers, as critics of this persuasion came to be known, contended that the school system has become a closed institution that is able to monopolize and control education by defining education as a set of activities that can only occur in schools. Society today does not recognize learning unless it is certified by a school. Furthermore, although they are expected to reduce social inequalities, schools instead legitimate them. The disadvantaged remain disadvantaged, despite compensatory treatments, because failure is built into the system; indeed, failure is required as a mechanism for the efficient distribution of social and economic status.

As creatures of the dominant system, according to the critique, schools alone cannot create the conditions for a more equal society. Efforts to reform society which focus on the schools while leaving the dominant political and economic structures intact are deemed to be futile. The problems of equality and justice are further compounded in that schools themselves have proved to be unamenable to fundamental change. The institutionalization, professionalization, and bureaucratization of schools cause them to adopt as a major (albeit unofficial) policy objective their own survival as an institution. Thus, with schools, as constituted, unable to produce social equality and unable to be changed as an institution, the only solution was to deschool society, that is, to broaden and redefine what is meant by education and to develop alternatives for learning that did not depend on the traditional schooling system.

Perhaps the greatest achievement of the deschoolers was to challenge the widely-held assumption that educational progress meant getting more people into more schools for longer periods of time. Their great weakness, however, lay in their inability to suggest alternatives that were as useful as their criticism. In the words of Ian Lister, who was prominent among the deschoolers, 'it was easier to criticize existing systems than to show ways beyond them' (Lister, 1976).[13]

While the deschoolers delivered a functional analysis of the schools in society, another branch of criticism focused on the developmental and educational implications of schooling. An influential study of schools in the United States, for example, found most classrooms to be 'joyless' places, intellectually sterile and aesthetically barren (Silberman, 1973).[14] The emphasis on control of 'pupil personnel', on managerial efficiency and production values, said the critics, acted to crush individuality, spontaneity, and creativity. School environments were compared to factories and even prisons. Perhaps the most damaging effect of the 'incarceration' of students in these 'minimum security prisons' (Brown, 1973)[15] is the crippling of their ability to mature properly. Prolonging the period of school attendance through adolescence was seen to keep young people in a 'condition of infantile dependence' (Reed and Bazalgette, 1977)[16] at a time when they should be maturing socially through interaction with the adult world. Efforts to improve or 'humanize' the institutional environment of schools were believed to do nothing, moreover, to alleviate the isolation and dependence fostered by school life. Schools merely provide 'academic playpens where the young can develop their own cultures and live out extended childhoods' (Lister, 1976).[17]

Thus, instead of being prepared for, or integrated into society whole cohorts of young adults are kept apart from and out of it, placed like Indians in reservations; confined in their own game-parks to play their own games; kept off the streets and out-of-town, in remote campuses. Sadly, for many of these might be seen as open prisons, and for many, walls are unnecessary because there is nowhere (in the economy) for them to go. (Lister, 1976)

The critics, who focused on the debilitating effects on young people of school life and the absence of real-life experiences, helped call attention to a grave defect in schooling as conventionally practised: young people are expected to prepare for the challenges and complexities of adult life without participating in significant activities. Thus, 'the final act of school-leaving is not experienced so much as a launching into the adult world in company with one's fellow students, but much more like a crumbling off at the edge. . . . It is something which happens to them, forced on them from outside rather than something they manage for themselves' (Reed and Bazalgette, 1977).[18]

Attempts have thus been made in some countries to develop educational schemes that meet the broader developmental needs of young people, in particular those that relate to a successful transition to adulthood. In the United States, for example, the Panel on Youth of the President's Science Advisory Committee, chaired by James S. Coleman, released a report that recommended 'the introduction of roles other than the student for a young person in school' and 'innovations which involve a mixture of part-time school and part-time work'. The report suggested two classes of objectives relating to the transition from youth to adulthood: objectives that are self-centred, that is, those that expand the personal capabilities, and thus opportunities, of individual young people; and objectives that relate the individual to others, that is, which provide the opportunity for 'the mutually responsible and mutually rewarding involvement with others that constitutes social maturity.' Included in this second class of objectives is 'experience with persons differing in social class, subculture and age,' 'the experience of having others dependent on one's actions,' and 'involvement in interdependent activities directed towards common goals' (Coleman, 1974).

The critiques of schooling we have just described were generated during a time of social and political turmoil, much of it centered in the young populations of the industrialized countries. Widespread dissatisfaction with schools, as articulated by these critiques, gave rise to attempts to develop alternative educational programmes that would avoid the weaknesses and offences of the established systems. Many of these alternatives proved to be short-lived, perhaps in some cases, as Lister has suggested, because a strong aversion by their originators to institutionalization caused them to 'under-institutionalize' their projects and deprive them thereby of a strong base. Their failure to become established made them vulnerable and expendable; when school budgets began to tighten in the late 1970s they often lost their funding. 'This gives rise,' as Lister has noted, 'to a sober thought that, in Western society, deschooling and alternatives were features of an economic boom rather than of an economic crisis' (Lister, 1976).[20]

Recent developments on the world economic scene have profoundly affected both the young and their schools, and have served to underscore the closeness with which schools are tied to the economic system. The emerging concern with broader issues of youth development and the successful transition to satisfying adulthood which was the legacy of the years of criticism has given way to a narrower, more pragmatic concern with transition from school to the workplace. Economic developments have produced two kinds of forces, with schools caught in the middle. First, a fiscal contraction has both inflated the schools' role in determining who gets work, and it has decreased their ability to assure their graduates a place in the job market. This situation, in turn, has unleashed a counterforce that manifests itself in changing attitudes among young people towards both education and work. As analyzed by Torsten Husén in an OECD report prepared for the Ministerial Conference on Youth Unemployment, the changing attitudes are both a cause and a consequence of the 'malaise' which pervades the educational systems of the highly industrialized countries in the late 1970s (Husén, 1978).[21]

During the 1960s, expenditures on education increased twice as fast as did GNP, while the elimination of economic and geographic obstacles and the development of mass education enhanced opportunities for further education. Together they produced a 'revolution of rising expectations' among young people in the less-privileged classes: formal equality of access to education was expected to lead to equality of life chances – notwithstanding the subsequent contrary arguments by deschoolers.

In the 1970s, however, expenditures on education declined for demographic reasons and the economic recesssion confirmed or aggravated an already familiar phenomenon: more graduates than jobs. Young people found that their degrees led only to unemployment or, at best, to poorly-paid jobs previously held by people with less education.

At the same time, the 'status-distributive' function of the educational system was reinforced, as the extension of compulsory basic education allowed the labour market to delegate the sorting function to schools and universities. The resulting obsessive concern with grades, examinations, and diplomas, according to Husén, tends to distort basic educational values and to prevent the educational system from functioning adequately. Particularly neglected are the 'less tangible objectives such as initiative, independent study, the ability to work together and to take responsibility.' Greater competition leads to a dichotomy, in prestige and employment opportunities, between those who have successfully completed particular types of training or levels of study and 'the others'.

Students at both ends of the academic spectrum are victimized by this pattern. Those who receive high marks are ready to prolong their studies, even when their attitudes about their schooling are quite negative, so as not to lose their advantage for employment and social advancement. Whether the study and the career it leads to are really in line with the interests of the student is often a secondary matter. Meanwhile, the losers in the academic race – early school-leavers with low qualifications (or none at all), most of whom are from underprivileged homes – are extremely negative in their attitudes toward both school and work.

Taking note of student protests against marks and exams and their claims for greater participation in decision making, Husén says it is possible to discern what might be called a 'silent revolution' among students, inspired by values which have led to a redefinition of work, of success, and of the quality of life. The new attitudes are characterized by a number of distinguishing views:

Education is not intended to develop vocational skills alone, but the whole personality;
The notion of working for marks on a relative scale, where the able and ambitious succeed and the others fail, has been rejected

in favour of trying to acquire useful and lasting skills;
There is active resistance among young people to the spirit of
competition and the cult of diplomas, in favour of delayed
occupational choices and studies combined with a career;
New importance is attached to personal fulfilment, security, and
rewarding leisure activities, with a narrowing gap between
privileged and poorer groups.

Two Case Studies

What is the impact of these social trends and conditions on the lives
of individual young people? To help answer this question, we offer
descriptions of two typical young people: Wendy, a 17-year-old
living in Toronto, Canada; and Jan, a 16-year-old from Amsterdam,
Holland.[22]

Wendy. Wendy, 17, lives with her mother, a kindergarten
teacher, brother, 12, and sister, 15, in a large Canadian city. She
goes to an inter-city high school which prides itself on high academic
standards. She is quiet and shy. Her social life revolves around a
circle of girls she sees in school. After school they disperse to various
parts of the city, and although she talks to them on the phone she
sees very little of them outside of school. She's an average student in
a college-preparatory programme and quite conscientious about her
school work. She's most interested in English and likes to read. A
good deal of her time is spent at home with her younger brother and
sister. She watches a lot of television – hockey games, situation
dramas, and special shows – averaging 15—20 hours per week. Her
mother often overhears her children talking about families and
thinks they are talking about the lives of real people, only to discover
it's really a TV series. Her mother is busy with her work and does
not participate in any activities in the immediate neighborhood or
larger community – nor do any of her children. Wendy isn't very
happy or satisfied with her life during the school year. She worries
about exams and assignments and isn't really interested in any of her
subjects but English. She tended to be more pleased with her
situation when she was in the first years of high school than she is at
present (her senior year). She's happiest during the summer when
she goes to her family's cottage on a lake. At the lake, she reads,
swims, sunbathes and has some friends her age, including boyfriends.

At school, the boys she's interested in aren't interested in her. She tried to get part-time work – not for the money but to break up the boredom but couldn't find anything that would fit in with her schedule. She did get a part-time job as a waitress during the summer after high school.

Postscript. This brief description was written during Wendy's last year in high school. She is now in her second year in residence at a college 100 miles from her home. She wanted to take a programme in university that would lead to a job and enrolled in an early childhood education course in order to become a nursery school teacher. In this course, she has to major in (read) psychology. She finds she doesn't like psychology and won't have any chance to work with children until her last two years. She isn't sure she 'wants to teach young kids for the rest of her life' and has decided to drop out of university at the end of this year. Her only contact with young children has come through discussions of her mother's teaching and occasional days spent at her mother's kindergarten classroom. Her outlook on the future is not very hopeful and she's frequently depressed.

Jan. Jan lives in Amsterdam, Holland. Energetic and occasionally aggressive, Jan was stamped as a 'problem child' early in his school career for his stubborn refusal to submit to school discipline. By the end of his ten years of compulsory schooling, he was considered – and he considered himself – to be a failure at school. At the age of 16 he must face the fact that his schooling has prepared him neither academically nor practically. He has no job skills, and no idea what he wants to do next. Jan has the good fortune to live with parents who care for him, although his mother suffers from an illness that keeps her bedridden. But his father has been an unskilled labourer all his life, having drifted from job to job, and is in no position to advise Jan as to what to do with his life.

For a short time after he left school, Jan had a job unloading fruit at a local market, but when the growing season ended, so did the job. Since then he has spent most of his time with others his own age, 'hanging out' in the neighbourhood, drinking and getting high, occasionally fighting with another group of youths. Jan was with some friends one night when they broke the window of a shoe store. The experience frightened him, and he decided to try to find some new friends. But soon afterward, he was caught breaking into a cigarette-vending machine. In the process of examining the consequences of this action, he discovered that young people who are in trouble with the law in Holland can avoid going to a penal institution if they are in some type of regular school.

Jan then learned of a school in his community that, according to friends, was supposed to help him figure out what he wanted to do in life. He had little taste for further 'real' school, but he discovered that this place allowed him to spend at least two days a week away from the school in an adult work environment. So he found himself once again enrolled as a full-time student, joining about 100 other young people between the ages of 16 and 18. He was immediately placed in a small group of about 15 other young people, where he heard a lot of talk about self-reliance, vocational choices and responsibility . . .

At first glance, one might find it difficult to imagine two people as different from each other as Wendy and Jan. And yet these two young people have in common a predicament which they share with many young people throughout the industrialized world.

First, they are isolated from the adult world. Besides their parents, the only other adults with whom they come into contact regularly have been teachers. Both parents and teachers relate to them as authority figures. There is no opportunity to see them in other roles: teachers' private lives are concealed from students, and children seldom even see their parents at work, let alone participate in it. Like many young people, Jan joined a society, or subculture, of his peers, whose boundaries are set and whose norms are determined by its separation from, or even opposition to, the adult world. Adults often interpret the existence of the peer culture as young people's rejection of society, failing to recognize the extent to which youngsters feel themselves to have been rejected by a society which provides no meaningful roles for them.

Although Wendy is less involved in the peer culture than are many young people, a good deal of her time is spent being passively entertained. Watching and listening to television, radio, movies, and records is a major activity – an activity characterized by its passivity and by what some observers describe as vicarious participation in life. Time she spends at school is equally passive: mostly Wendy is listening to teachers talking, presumably being prepared for action that will occur some time in the future.

Most young people have little opportunity to learn about the world of work. Although Wendy was able to observe teachers at work, it was still difficult for her to know whether she would like to teach. For most occupations, students do not have even this limited exposure. As Jan discovered, moreover, the family is increasingly unable to provide the kind of career guidance that was possible in a less specialized age. Working parents are now more apt to have narrow, specialized skills that limit both their own knowledge of and their children's exposure to other options. As new careers emerge and familiar ones disappear, the knowledge that parents have of occupational choices may rapidly become obsolete. Although part-time work for young people is available in some countries, the jobs are often tailored exclusively for them – for example, work in fast-food restaurants in North America. Such jobs do not provide experience in adult work, and often amount to an extension of the youth culture. Most young people have only a limited notion of what they can do or would want to do occupationally.

The inability of Jan's parents to guide him in choosing a career points to another feature of the adolescent condition: the weakening of the family as society's primary socializing agent. Another sign is that Wendy's parents are divorced, an increasingly common phenomenon. But these are only part of a broader trend which Urie Bronfenbrenner, Professor of Human Development and Family Studies at Cornell University in the United States, describes as 'a "withering away" of the support systems in the larger society that . . . enable the family to function.' Among other factors contributing to this general breakdown, Bronfenbrenner mentions the fragmentation of the extended family, occupational mobility, the separation of residential from business and work areas, separate patterns of social life for different age groups, the disappearance of neighbourhoods, and child labour laws.

Perhaps the most critical aspect of their condition which Jan and Wendy have in common is the lack of opportunity to participate in society meaningfully. Their efforts are neither needed nor valued by the communities in which they live. According to a developmental psychologist, John J. Mitchell of the University of Alberta in Canada, the enforced idleness of youth denies a fundamental need of adolescents: the need to contribute:

The adolescent must give; he must build; he must construct; he must register impact upon his social and physical environment;

he must feel a sense of meaningful involvement in the significant events of his personal world. To ask the adolescent to live his day-to-day existence without contributing is to ask him to behave contrary to his basic makeup. (Mitchell, 1975, pp. 1-2)[23]

Young people have different ways of responding to this situation. Inclined toward conformity, Wendy tried to go along with what seemed to be expected of her, but finally became depressed and dropped out. More action-oriented, Jan escaped the confines of the school earlier (more a push-out than a drop-out) and sought other outlets for his energies. His involvement in destructive and criminal behaviour was practically inevitable, given his frustrated needs, as Mitchell explains:

The best way to insure that young people get into trouble is to design their environment so that non-troublesome behavior does not make a difference. Strip them of the ability to make a difference legally and they will find ways to make a difference illegally. Making a difference is far more important than efficiency, harmony, smoothness of operation, and learning subject matter and writing lessons.

The description of Jan ended with his admission to a new kind of school that seemed to offer a way out of his predicament. This school, called De Groene School, was created expressly to allow its students to learn by participating in an adult workplace. It is a project of a special committee within the Dutch Ministry of Education, the Innovatie Commissie Participatie-Onderwijs, or the Innovation Committee for Learning by Participation, whose work is described at some length in the chapter by Leendert van den Bosch. In order to explicate the meaning of LBP, we turn now to a definition and conceptual framework.

A Conceptual Framework for Learning by Participation

As Wendy, Jan and too many of their peers are painfully aware, the period of youth in the modern world is largely one of wasted opportunities. This waste affects young people, who are prevented from gaining a sense of usefulness and meaningful participation in any social arena. But it also affects society, which deprives itself not only of the contributions that young people are eager to make in the present, but also of the opportunity to assure itself of a generation of young people fully prepared to take on adult roles and responsibilities. It is a thesis of this book that young people must be treated, not as a collection of problems to be treated by adults, but as a vital resource in meeting the needs of society. The authors believe that Learning by Participation offers a programmatic vehicle for developing this resource while enabling young people to participate in their own learning and growth.

LBP is a comprehensive mode of learning which offers a programmatic means of linking theory with practice – in contrast with conventional schooling which concentrates on theory or abstract learning and leaves the practical application strictly 'theoretical.' LBP also places theory and practice in a reciprocating relationship.

Before venturing our own definition of LBP, we must voice several caveats. First, while we consider that LBP approaches a general theory of learning more adequately than conventional school models of learning and instruction do, we do not claim it to be all-encompassing as a learning model. We readily acknowledge that many important and valuable learning activities take place outside of LBP, although we do maintain that some form of LBP should constitute a part of every learner's educational programme.

It is inevitable perhaps that any detailed definition of Learning by Participation will be taken to imply standards against which individual programmes must be judged. Such standards can indeed be valuable insofar as they suggest an ideal toward which LBP programmes might strive. The criteria set down in a definition can also serve as a guide in planning new programmes, thus encouraging the application of high standards. Finally, we hope that a definition will advance further development of the concept of LBP, both clarifying it and aiding in its application.

Proposing general criteria for LBP at this stage in its development also contains some dangers, however, particularly when they are addressed to an international readership. Although one function of a definition is to exclude by drawing boundaries, we do not wish to imply that we fail to recognize the value of programmes that do not meet every criterion of the definition. Many of the programmes described in this book, in fact, only partially fit our definition.

Rather, our purpose is to be *inclusive*, in the sense of attracting to our definition of LBP those programmes that already meet some criteria and may be encouraged to adopt others. Despite the fact that our definition is derived from our collective experience in working with and learning about programmes in several different countries, both our knowledge and many of the programmes themselves are still in a formative stage. As our own experience broadens and as programmes mature, we assume that our ideas concerning LBP will evolve and that our definition and conceptual framework will be refined accordingly. We must caution, therefore, that the definition set forth below is both ideal and tentative. It is ideal in the sense that it describes all the features that a fully developed LBP programme ought to have. It is tentative in that it will be refined and changed as knowledge and experience of LBP accumulate and evolve.

Definition

Learning by Participation is an *integrative process* that includes *participation in society*, *critical reflection* on that participation, and the relation of experiences to *theoretical knowledge*, while maximizing the participation of all learners in decision-making affecting both the programme as a whole and their own individual activities in the programme.

A. Participation in society

Fundamental to LBP is that students learn by taking part actively in society. Participation means, firstly, that students exercise real responsibility: they make decisions that affect others besides themselves, they are held accountable for their actions, and they are able to experience the consequences of their actions, both success and failure. Participation means, secondly, that students engage in activities that are challenging, useful to others, and intrinsically rewarding.

B. Critical reflection.

LBP provides students with an opportunity to reflect critically on the outcomes, significance, and consequences of their participation. That is, they examine the meaning of their activities, both individually and as a group.

C. Theoretical knowledge.

Students relate both the practical experience of participation and their critical reflections on that experience to theoretical knowledge.

D. Integrative process.

These three dimensions are joined in an *integrative process* or cycle of learning which might be represented in the following manner:

Figure 1

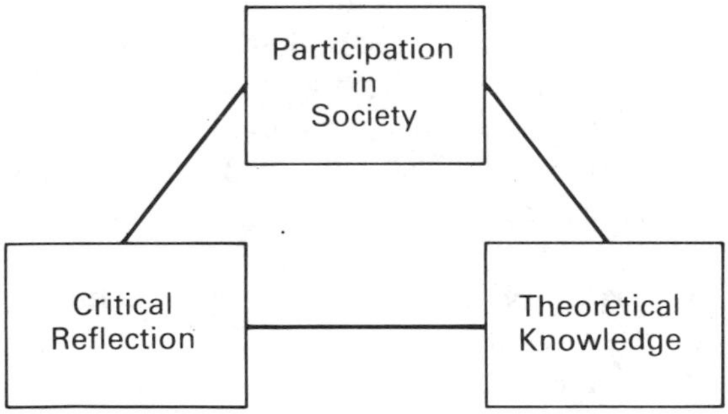

E. Decision making.

LBP is further enhanced insofar as students participate in planning, developing, operating, and evaluating their over-all programme, and insofar as each student can participate in decisions concerning his or her own learning activities.

Let us now examine these components in greater detail:

A. Participation in society.

This cornerstone of LBP means essentially that youth take part in important activities that entail real responsibility and that make a needed contribution to the community. The possibilities of what young people actually can do are indeed endless, limited only by constraints on the imagination and such practical limitations as may exist in local settings.

Individually, young people can work alongside an adult 'mentor,' learning what that work entails by doing it. At the same time, young people in such a mentorship arrangement establish a personal relationship with an adult and learn first-hand about life in a particular adult environment. Examples of adult mentors include carpenters, photographers, social service workers, teachers, storekeepers, health professionals, scientists, zookeepers, restaurant cooks, lawyers, and many others.

Students may also participate and learn in group activities. Once again, the possibilities are as numerous as are unmet social needs. Groups of young people can do urban conservation work, assist handicapped children, operate a farm, organize a food-buying cooperative, restore historic buildings, conduct health campaigns in poverty areas, make art displays for public show, provide shopping services for old people, and so forth. Sometimes adults are unable to think of community needs that young people might need. It does not matter; among the most successful programmes are many which rely on the students themselves to identify areas of need and to determine the course of action they will take.

One such program originated in a community studies program at Hillary college, a local secondary school in the suburb of Otara in South Auckland (New Zealand), an industrial area where vandalism and petty crime by young people is not uncommon. In 1973, a fourth form class (14 year olds) began to look at the social needs of their suburb, which has thousands of low-cost public housing developments for low-income families, mostly Maoris or Pacific Islanders. Their teacher helped the class to devise a program of surveys and a study of town planning and local government. The pupils developed the idea that what Otara needed most was a centrally situated recreation center, which could serve as a place to hold indoor sports, a drop-in center, and a focus for a wide range of community cultural activities. They promoted the idea in the local media and talked to a number of community groups.

The idea caught the imagination of local people. It received nationwide media coverage and the support of central government legislators, who offered a generous subsidy if the community would raise some of the necessary funds. The community moved behind the project and raised enough money so that the community center, called '*Te Puke O Tara*,' a Maori name, opened in 1976. (Norman, 1977, pp. 42—5)[24]

Our definition of participation places special emphasis on responsibility. This is based on a belief that one learns to act responsibly by having, and exercising, responsibility. The argument is often heard that responsibility must be *earned*, as if it comes as a reward for demonstrating that one is 'ready.' Much schooling, accordingly, is said to aim at 'preparing' the young for the responsibility they presumably will assume at some future time. In contrast, we believe that responsibility must be *learned*, and that one learns it by experiencing it. We also believe, based on abundant evidence (much of it reported in this book), that young people are ready for a great deal more responsibility than they are generally given credit for, and that when the resposibility is real they take it very seriously.

The responsibility must be real. One test of real responsibility is that others are dependent on one's actions, that is, that one's actions and decisions have an effect on people other than oneself. Another dimension of responsibility is that one is held accountable for what one does. There is a tendency for adults to protect the young from possible negative consequences of their actions. Whatever their motives, in doing this adults cheat young people of an invaluable lesson, one they need in order to mature. The definition of LBP stresses, therefore, that responsibility requires that learners must experience the consequences of their actions, and that this includes the right to fail and to learn from one's mistakes. Of course, this also means that one has the right to succeed, and to experience the sweet reward of feeling truly responsible for one's success. 'It is precisely the acceptance of responsibility,' according to Silberman (1975, p. 597) 'that breeds a sense of ownership or proprietorship in one's society, a sense of autonomy, independence, and control over one's environment.'

In addition to emphasizing responsibility, our definition of participation lays down certain standards regarding the activities that learners carry out. First, they should be challenging, which is to say difficult and not easy to do. The activities should cause learners to stretch and test their capacities beyond what they can currrently do. Second, the activities should be socially useful, that is, they should be of real benefit to others, not just the learner alone. This allows young people to fulfil their need to make a contribution to society, to make a difference in their environment. Many 'hands-on' or learning-by-doing programmes omit this dimension – for example, training programmes in which young people learn to operate machines, or simulation programmes. The test of participation in this instance is whether the activity has a social, not just personal, impact. Take as an example a high school science class that undertook to design and build a windmill as part of a study of alternative energy sources. If the purpose were limited to learning outcomes for the students, then it would not be LBP by our defintion, even though students learned a great deal. In this case, however, the windmill was put to use, providing power needed by an agricultural project at the same school. Thus it met LBP's standard of social usefulness.

The third standard is that the activities should be intrinsically rewarding; that is, they should be worth doing for their own sake. This criterion encompasses a wide range of possible developmental benefits. For example, the learner might gain in learning to act independently, or in a group, or in making decisions, or in being exposed to a whole new segment of society such as an urban transportation system or a home for the aged. It might also be noted that while LBP experiences might well have value in exposing students to work-skills, the primary learning aim entaiis a much broader conception of personal growth and development. The criterion that learning experiences must be intrinsically motivating is in contrast with most school work, which is considered extrinsically rewarding in that the real value of the learning activity is only realized later in life. Because schools, typically, do not consider it necessary that students find the learning process itself rewarding, they provide surrogate or artificial incentives like grades and awards (to say nothing of negative sanctions and punishments).

The demand that LBP activities must be challenging and rewarding tends to rule out drudge work such as cleaning sheets or stuffing envelopes, even though these activities may be socially useful. It is conceivable that activities such as these could form part of a larger project that also included more interesting work, but they should not be the dominant activity.

In general, students find LBP experiences worthwhile when they feel their actions are considered important by others, whether these be individuals, as for instance when a youth tutors a younger child, or the larger community, when young people provide a needed service. This action is vividly illustrated by Alex Dickson, who is the creator of Great Britain's Community Service Volunteers. He is fond of telling the following story about an English school, Brierly Road Secondary Modern School, Crewe.

Kids leave this school in great numbers at the earliest age they can. In fact, they are kicking at the door to get out into what they believe to be 'real life.' And in a recent class of thirty-two, sixteen were involved professionally with the local probation officer.

An imaginative teacher arranged one day to take his whole class to the local hospital. There, confronting them, were nine children with congenital spinal injury – children in whom a kind of hinge mechanism in the bottom of the spine has been 'cranked up' at birth. Unless there is a particularly intelligent and successful operation, they deform pretty quickly. There is not much that surgery or medicine can do after that.

But here they were, unable to move, terribly immobile. The nurses had to lift them, to feed them, to toilet them, to put them to bed, and to attend to their every need. When Mom takes the kid home, she becomes the prisoner of her own child.

Then these difficult 15 year-old kids were told, 'What you see here is a technological problem – they can't move. Do you think you can help them?'

Back at the school, in the workshop, they wrestled with the problem. What material could best be used? What design? In seven weeks' time, they returned to the hospital, led by their head-master. They handed over nine beautifully polished, boomerang-shaped trays to take the splayed-out legs of each child. The trays were mounted on caster wheels, an inch and a half off the ground, so that each kid with his fingertips could propel himself in any direction across the floor.

When the trays were handed over, the children's mothers were in tears. The children themselves were euphoric; the hospital staff was astounded, and the 15 year-olds were strangely silent. The headmaster himself was moved by the impact this evidently made on his difficult young people. He asked a probing question, and got two classically beautiful answers. Why had this made such an impact on them? The first answer was: 'Because it's the first bloody thing we made in school that we didn't have to take home afterwards.' But the second was: 'Because nobody said it was good for us. They said it was serious, dead serious'.[26]

LBP has a social as well as a personal dimension because students work with people in the community and carry out activities that benefit society. Another social dimension of great importance is participation in a group effort toward a common goal. LBP programmes offer the opportunity to interact cooperatively with both peers and people of different ages, in sharp contrast to the excessively individualized and competitive climate of most schooling. Many young people have little or no experience with such social processes as group decision-making, problem-solving, team work, communication and collaboration in situations where their actions will affect their group and others. These experiences are most directly provided by LBP programmes in which all the participants work toward the same clearly defined goal, such as identifying sources of water pollution, renovating a historic church, creating a public work of art, or constructing a windmill.

Similar experiences may also be acquired, however, in programmes in which learners are placed individually in community settings. In these cases the common goals are those of the workplace, and students share them with the adults there. It is important, of course, that the students enter the social processes that constitute the group effort. A student who works at an infant care centre, for example, works collaboratively with full-time workers in providing services to children; a young person who works with a cook in a cafeteria learns the interdependence required to provide meals for large numbers of people.

Other opportunities for group decision-making occur during student participation in the programme, as discussed below, in part E.

B. Critical reflection.

Experience alone does not automatically produce learning. Students must have an opportunity to reflect critically on the outcomes, significance and consequences of their participation. This aspect of LBP helps them translate their raw experience from the field into a form whose meaning they can interpret, which they can relate to their own lives, and which they can relate to theoretical knowledge and conceptual reasoning. Reflection involves the ability to make intelligent observations, collect data and make written and verbal reports on one's experience, and to analyze the process and the content of that experience.

The two most commonly-used methods for ensuring learning in this mode are the keeping of a journal and moderated group discussions. Journals provide students with a means for recording the occurrences of their experiences as well as their immediate reflections on them. They may be narrative and impressionistic or they may be structured in a variety of ways, depending on the learning needs and objectives. CAEL (Cooperative Assessment of Experiential Learning), a joint project of Educational Testing Services and a group of U.S. colleges and universities, recommends a log format having four sections. In section one, the student merely writes down the events of particular interest in each day of experiential learning activity. Next, the student describes those thoughts, ideas, concepts, and questions which have grown out of the experiences. The third and fourth sections allow for additional reactions from the log analyst and the student (CAEL, 1975, p. 13).

If journals are, at least initially, an individualized mode of observation and reflection, discussions are a way of expanding one's perceptions of experience through group sharing. Students whose participatory activity takes them to separate day care centres, for example, gain new insights into their experience through telling others about it and contrasting it with others' accounts. There are, of course, other ways to sharpen one's awareness of what one is experiencing. Observations may be structured in advance through a data-gathering task; interviews may be conducted with adults involved; group-process techniques such as role-play and problem-solving may be used to supplement discussions.

A programme in California (United States) illustrates one possible approach to the critical reflection mode. In this programme, 15 young people (aged 15—17) worked several days each week in individual placements in the community. One student worked in a day care centre, for example, while another worked in the local office of a legislator in state government, and another worked in a social welfare agency. Once a week all 15 students met in a two-hour 'seminar' to reflect on their experiences in their work settings. In the course of these sessions, which were led by two adult programme directors, the students learned to describe their work activities and articulate their meaning, to experiment with different roles through role-play, to take responsibility for their own actions, to recognize and express their own needs, and to defend their own values. The students each analyzed their individual roles in their work settings, and were encouraged to think about how they grew as a result of their experiences – for instance, gaining self-confidence, feeling more comfortable with adults, learning to cope with unexpected situations, and thinking more clearly about the future.

In planning the seminars, the programme leaders addressed themselves analytically to two aspects of the work or 'internship' experience: what they call the *process* of involvement, that is, how the internship affects the students personally; and the *content* of the experience, that is, what may be learned about the agencies where they work, and thus about the community they live in. In practice in the seminars these two aspects overlapped considerably, both often being dealt with in the same exercise. In one sample exercise the students were asked to describe the social use of space at their work settings. First, drawing floor plans, they mapped out the physical location, indicating where each person worked, had a desk, or spent time. These relative placements of people were then analyzed to see what they said about the relationships, both formal and informal – for example, lines of authority and subordination, patterns of communication, and relation to the work task. Finally, students were asked to 'place' themselves in the organization, and to analyze, within the supportive context of their peers and adult leaders, the effect others had on them and their own impact on their individual settings.

In the seminar discussions, young people often identify information they need in order to complete tasks they have assumed at their work settings. For example, those working on a project to remove architectural barriers for the physically handicapped need to know specifications for ramps, what they cost, how they are installed, the proper incline, and so on. Often this information is learned on the job, but when it is not, seminar participants can be helped to identify what they need to know and to learn where to obtain needed information.

Another function of the critical-reflection phase of LBP is for young people to gain perspective on the socio-historical context of their participation location. That is to say, students do not confine their examinations to the internal workings of their community placement sites. Rather, they also evaluate the conditions they encounter in their work settings in relation to issues and concerns in the broader society. In addition, they explore the implications of their own experience for what it can teach them about their own role in that society. Thus, critical reflection serves a mediating role, helping students to see the relationship of both themselves and their studies to the community of which they are members.

C. *Theoretical knowledge.*

Learning by Participation, according to our model, should enable students to relate the practical experience of their participation, and their reflection on that participation, to theoretical knowledge and abstract reasoning. In this phase of learning, the individual detaches himself or herself from concrete experience, but draws on actual observations and specific data in order to derive generalizations and general principles.

Through participation in society and reflection on their experience, students are motivated to seek the knowledge they need in order to be more effective, rather than passively receive knowledge that meets no immediately felt need, as school expects of them. In this phase, then, students might carry out library or field research on topics related to their experience, or write papers that integrate their experience with existing knowledge. Students whose activities involve helping the mentally retarded, for example, could explore the physical or medical causes of retardation, the history of treatment of the retarded, local provisions for serving the retarded population, and how those provisions relate to their psychological needs, social policy concerning the retarded (institutional- versus neighbourhood-based care), and so forth. Alternatively, the same students could do photo-essays, stories, journalistic reports, plays or videotapes on the retarded. Similar types of knowledge-consolidating activities could take place, of course, for almost any participatory experience.

It is also possible to relate experience to conventional subject disciplines. A programme in which students do construction work in the community, for example, or take ecological defence action, can readily use the field experience as a basis to learn reading and writing, mathematics, science, social studies and other academic subjects. The same is true, moreover, whether the study is elementary or advanced. The important principle of LBP here is that the theoretical knowledge should grow out of the concrete experience which precedes it. The two then mutually enrich and reinforce each other, usually mediated by critical reflection.

Using concrete experience to motivate and direct knowledge-seeking often has the effect, desired by many educators, of bridging the artificial boundaries between disciplines. This allows academic study to become more responsive to social situations, which generally do not fit into the narrow confines of academic disciplines. This social dimension of knowledge-seeking enables students to look deeply into the established fields of theoretical knowledge and to evaluate how they relate to real-world problems. In acquiring theoretical knowledge and then applying it back in their participation activities, students come to see knowledge as an *active* phenomenon with great power for being effective and doing good.

The fact that LBP bases learning on practical experience by no means constitutes a devaluing of the type of learning associated with schools. On the contrary, it is essential to cognitive development. Coleman (1970)[28] observes that because school-type learning relies on a symbolic medium it can enormously reduce the time and effort necessary to learn. The collective knowledge and insights of mankind can be crystallized into a form that is transmitted to young people, who are thus spared the recapitulation of the total experience of mankind themselves. Further, such learning helps them to develop the capacity to generate principles which can be applied in new and unique situations.

Using cross-cultural investigations where excessive schooling had not yet become a cultural value, Scribner and Cole (1973, p. 554)[29] found that 'unschooled populations tended to solve individual problems singly, each as a new problem, whereas schooled populations tended to treat them as instances of a class of problems that could be solved by a general rule.' In other words, schooling gives the young the capacity to synthesize specific problems into general and abstract problem-sets, whereas non-schooled populations usually focus on concrete and task-specific learning. Concrete learning is like most of non-school learning and must be joined with abstract learning if its full potential is to be realized. It does not necessarily follow, however, that schooling is imperative for abstract cognitive development to occur. In their studies of traditional cultures, Scribner and Cole showed how out-of-school formal learning provided many learning possibilities, both concrete and abstract. There is no reason this should be different in our own modern culture.

D. *Integrative process.*

LBP may be seen as a cyclical process that integrates different modes of learning. Two features must be present for it to function effectively. First, the learning process is most productive when the three components – participation in society, critical reflection, and abstraction – interact reciprocally, or, cyclically. Second, the cycle should be completed in a relatively brief time-period, followed by a new cycle. That is, the engagement of one component by another, followed by another, and so forth, is an ongoing process by which the components are integrated into a continuous learning cycle. This repeating process results in what may be called a 'spiral of learning'.

Conventional schooling fails to provide a 'spiral of learning' in this sense because it is linear in nature and follows a quite different learning sequence. Coleman (1976),[30] for example, has suggested that schools follow a four-step sequence consisting of (1) giving information through a symbolic medium, (2) assimilating and organizing information so that some general principle is understood, (3) inferring a particular application from the general principle, and (4) moving to the sphere of action. In actuality, the sequence which Coleman outlines is rarely completed in school. Only after years of information gathering, symbolic processing, and cognitive orienting in school are young people sent into the world to begin the phase of action, or the application in life, of the things learned at school. It requires the whole of schooling and beyond to complete this cycle, which thereby becomes essentially linear in nature. Further, because the phase of action is assumed to take place after young people leave school, it is questionable if the cycle is ever genuinely completed.

LBP follows quite a different pattern from that which typifies conventional schooling. Beginning with concrete experience, it moves quickly to the critical-reflection phase, which both clarifies the experience and points the way to related theoretical knowledge. Abstract learning that is rooted in an action experience deepens and enriches the significance of the experience, the understanding of which is enhanced through further reflection.

Let us take an example, based on a field observation by one of the authors (Dollar). A young woman is in an LBP programme in which students build houses – one a year – which are then sold to poor families for the cost of the building materials (which finances the building of next year's house). This young woman has specialized in carpentry, although she has also learned plumbing, roofing, and electrical wiring. The curriculum of her mathematics class has been designed to be coordinated with her experience on the job. She and the three other student-carpenters have just discovered that their supply of boards has been cut too short for the dimensions of the room they are working on. In their weekly seminar the next day, the students discuss solutions to their problem. After telephoning their lumber supplier, they learn that they cannot return the boards because they have already accepted them. Can they afford to buy new boards? Can they alter the design of the room? Can they use boards from a different part of the house? The suggestion is finally made that there may be enough wood in the boards they have to finish the job if some of them are cut in pieces that can be used to lengthen the others. They are not structural boards and they will not be visible when the house is completed, so it seems like a possible solution. The unanswered question is whether there is enough wood, or how much more will be needed. The teacher who is moderating their discussion knows that this is exactly the kind of problem that the building experience is supposed to raise. He suggests that the students ask in their next mathematics class the best way to get a answer to their question. The students complain that they will have to wait an extra day for that.

E. Student decision-making: Participation in the programme.

Students may make decisions in their programmes at two levels, the programme level and the individual level. At the programme level students make collective decisions that affect what they do, what they study, and how they do these things. The decisions in which they take part determine their activities as a group. At the individual level, each student is able to make decisions concerning his or her own activities and course of study.

Programme-level decisions, as we have mentioned, include participation in the planning, development, operation, and evaluation of the programme as a whole. A planning decision at the most basic level would be to determine the purpose of the programme itself. An LBP programme might begin, for example, with a study by young people of community needs. This could be a rather elaborate group participation activity in itself, involving surveys of community opinions, interviews with representative officials and citizens, research in the local library and newspaper, and so forth. The objective would be to focus on a number of social problems or community needs on which the students might take action. The problems might include local air or water pollution, or the needs of home-bound old people (food, transportation, house repairs, companionship, etc.), or consumer information needs. Students would decide collectively which problem to address, and then begin a process leading to a decision as to the proper action to take.

Let us assume that the students have decided to offer a service of home repairs to poor and aged people. Participating in the development of the programme might include determining how to locate eligible recipients of the repairs, how much time each student will be expected to work, and what kinds of repairs will be provided. Decisions concerning the programme's operation could include which repair jobs to take, how to deal with the costs of materials and tools, and what to do when a student's attendance is poor. Students can also take part in group decisions regarding the reflective and academic sides of their LBP programme. Participation in evaluation of the programme means that students assess the effectiveness of their programme, identify problem areas, and make decisions leading to the programme's improvement. Admittedly, it is rare for a single programme to offer a full range of decision-making opportunities in all these areas. Often, for instance, it is necessary to specify exactly what students will be doing in order for a programme to be officially approved. Whatever the constraints, however, we must maintain that, *educationally* speaking, the more opportunities exist for student decision-making the greater the benefit as a learning and growing experience.

Decision-making by the individual student on matters affecting his or her own programme is the other form of participation in the programme. The most basic of these decisions is whether to become involved in the LBP programme at all. Ideally, participation is voluntary and (soon) self-motivating. After that, programmes can be designed to maximize each student's control over his or her activities and learning programme. In programmes involving individual work-placement in the community, students can investigate and choose their own work site, perhaps after a series of interviews at the sites the students find most interesting. A student can then be responsible for negotiating the terms of his or her activity at the site – frequency and duration of work, content of activities, opportunity to carry responsibility, and the like. The student can also help decide how his or her performance will be evaluated. The reflective and academic phases of the programme pose other opportunities for individual decision-making. For example, choices may be offered for fulfilling academic requirements – a research paper, a special project carried out at the work site and described in writing, an oral report (the audience for which need not be limited to fellow students), and so on.

The idea of a greater voice in the course of one's own learning programme has gained favour along with the call for more individualization in education. These are necessary responses to the excesses of mass schooling, which include standardization, regimentation, and depersonalization. But in seeking to reassert the differentiated needs of individuals, one should not lose sight of another effect of mass schooling, which is to suppress students' interdependence. Both in school and out of school, young people rarely have an opportunity to interact cooperatively, or to work together for a common purpose. Group decision-making in an LBP programme is one way of having this developmentally critical experience. Therefore, occasions for individual decision-making should not be multiplied at the expense of those for making group decisions. Rather, the importance of both should be recognized and a balance be struck between the two.

The opportunity to make decisions is thus an important criterion in assessing the quality of a participation activity or experience for youth. These decisions can be broad, made in concert with adults and/or other young people, influencing general policies and directions. They may also be decisions made by the individual student in the course of his or her day-to-day activities. A student whose activities involve him or her in work at a day-care centre, for example, may take part with adults in collective decisions affecting services at the centre in general, such as setting guidelines for volunteer work by parents, or selecting games and play equipment for purchase by the centre. On the personal level, opportunities can be provided for the student to decide in advance upon what kind of activity he or she will perform as part of helping at the day-care centre. Another very important form of decision-making for young people to experience comes when unexpected situations arise that call for some immediate action, and the young person must decide what to do. In a day-care centre, this might mean deciding what to do when two children fight over a toy, or when a child withdraws from a group, or when parents do not arrive to fetch their children when expected.

To illustrate these different kinds of decisions and the opportunity to experience them, let us imagine two young people, William and Anne, whose LBP programme involves them in work with pre-school children in two different day-care centres. When William arrives at the centre where he works, he is given his assignment for the afternoon. Sometimes he is asked to watch the children while they play outside; sometimes he serves the afternoon snack; other times he cleans up after the children have finished finger-painting. His work frees the regular day-care teachers for other activities, but involves only a fraction of William's capabilities. Despite his pleasant demeanour, he is usually bored. Anne works at a different day-care centre, but under the condition that once a week she will plan and carry out an activity with a small group of children. Anne has invented many games to teach the children: one to help them distinguish colours, another to help them understand the concept of height. In the process of her work, Anne has developed a strong attachment to Charlie, a three-year-old who rarely speaks. In a seminar where she meets with his teacher and other young people who also work in day-care centres, Anne discusses ways of helping Charlie. In contrast to William, Anne feels she is expected to make a positive contribution to the centre. The adults there assume she is capable of acting intelligently and purposefully. Together with her relationship with Charlie, this makes Anne feel needed, and accounts for her strong commitment to her work at the centre.

Before leaving the subject of decision-making affecting the programme, a distinction should be drawn between decisions that are made by youth participants as a group and those that are made by youth *representatives*. It is a growing practice in some countries to place one or two young people on adult advisory or policy-making bodies at various official levels in order to give young people a voice in the programmes intended to serve them. Sometimes these are committees at the school level. Sometimes, too, councils are established made up entirely of young people, who then advise officials about the 'youth point of view.' Whatever the merits of these arrangements (and their merits vary widely from place to place), decisions made by young people representing larger numbers should not be mistaken for the participation in decision-making we are explaining here. In the former case, the point is that the interests of young people should be represented. In the latter, learning by participation, the point is that decision-making is an experience that *every* young person needs in order to develop and mature. One does not learn and grow through the action of one's representative.

In concluding this section, we might repeat that LBP is composed of two kinds of participation by students: participation in society and participation in their own programmes. The first kind is important because young people need to be able to make a difference in the real world outside the school; the second is important because they need to have a greater voice, both individually and collectively, in determining their own education in a system that is ostensibly intended to serve them. It is often maintained that schools cannot realistically be expected to begin meeting the needs of their clients as long as those clients (students) remain powerless, and unable to participate in decisions affecting their programme. It is also maintained that changing the educational system will not change society and that, in any case, real educational change is unlikely without prior changes in the broader social and economic systems. Taken together, these arguments raise sobering questions about the limits of educational reform. Yet precisely because it emphasizes the two kinds of participation, in which students learn both to have an impact on society and to gain a measure of power over their education, LBP may represent a feasible first step toward real change.

We have noted that interest is growing in forms of education that base learning on active involvement in the community. One hears increasingly about such innovative approaches as service learning, field studies, practicum, experiential education, and youth participation. The trend, as we indicated earlier, is not limited to the Western industrialized countries. The actual motives for involvement in participatory learning, however, are context specific. Many Third World countries have launched national programmes of 'study-service', which is a term applied to community service when it is an integral part of course work at an educational institution. Examples of study-service schemes at the university level include Nepal's National Development Service, Indonesia's *Kuliah Kerja Nyata* (KKN), Nigeria's National Youth Service Corps, and Ghana's National Service Scheme, all of which require students to spend up to one academic year in practical development work as part of their university courses. These programmes serve the dual purpose of (1) making a direct contribution to national development through the services rendered to clients, and (2) indirect benefit to the nation through the educational effect that this experience has on participants – most of whom will become the country's leaders, and who otherwise would have no personal contact with the realities of the development situation. Some countries also have similar programmes for secondary students. In Western Samoa, for example, in a school-sponsored programme called Channel College Volunteer Farm, village boys learn farming and encourage neighbours to improve their strains of livestock. The Tabora Girls' School in Tanzania involves its secondary students in literacy teaching, as does the Kasama Girls' Secondary School (Practical humanism course) in Zambia. And in El Salvador, the Diversified Student Service of the National Youth Movement recruits volunteers from secondary and vocational schools for community development and work in social service agencies (Woods, 1977).[31] Programmes such as these are gaining international support and recognition, both as an important form of education in themselves and as a tool to help bring about other changes in education. An example of this increasing support is that the General Conference of UNESCO in Nairobi in 1976 decided to commit UNESCO to helping the development of study-service, thus adding to the efforts that UNICEF has made in this field for some time.

A related educational approach that has gained favour in

developing countries in recent years is so-called non-formal education. This approach, a traditional form of learning in its own right, avoids the isolation and over-institutionalization of traditional schooling by systematically exploiting the learning opportunities in daily life. Its attractiveness grows out of a belief that formal schooling is too expensive for poorer countries to conduct on a mass scale. In addition, some consider schooling to be so tied to traditional attitudes, religious customs, and conservative forces in society that they do not constitute a sound investment for national development. In contrast, non-formal programmes have the flexibility and adaptability required to meet ever-changing national needs. They also promise more in terms of costs relative to formal schooling (Coombs, 1976).[32]

The socialist countries of Eastern Europe have long linked education with the life and labour of the working class. The very young are introduced to 'socially useful labour' from the time they begin schooling. 'Kindergartners' help care for the flowers and trees on the school grounds, while young primary-school children help build and maintain community swimming pools and playgrounds. The transition to socially useful productive labour as a part of all secondary schooling is thus smooth and natural. Especially after the reforms of 1958, which stressed the necessity of tying schools more closely to 'life,' all of Eastern Europe has reserved a portion of its secondary schooling programme for young people to engage in 'productive labour.' In addition to these school-based programmes, most countries have national organizations that involve young people in service projects. The National Council of Hungarian Youth, for example, organizes student brigades to perform construction work in less developed areas of Hungary, while the Institute of Health Education in Yugoslavia conducts a programme in which students work in health education, hygiene, and sanitation in less developed parts of that country.

The disparate efforts in various countries of the world to introduce participation into learning are mutually independent, and not part of any organized movement. Yet they do have some basic precepts in common, including the need – and the right – of a nation's young citizens to participate actively in society, and the value of participation in facilitating learning. In the Western industrialized countries, in particular, advocates of LBP appear to be motivated by similar perceptions of both the problem and the solution. These points of commonality make comparisons of LBP experiences in different countries especially valuable. The strategies and designs employed in one country can prove highly instructive to LBP planners and practitioners in another – as has been demonstrated in the course of exchanges that have already taken place among the countries represented in the chapters that follow. It is hoped that this book, by reporting on LBP activities in these countries, will serve not only to strengthen existing localized efforts to establish LBP, but also to lead eventually to their coalescing into a significant international movement.

The spirit of international collaboration is certainly present in this volume. The authors of the respective chapters were in close association with one another from the earliest stages of conception until the book's final completion. Thus, although each author was primarily responsible for his own chapter, the book must properly be considered as a joint product. The chapters all follow a similar outline. The authors explore the societal conditions in their respective regions which shape and give rise to Learning by Participation efforts. They discuss the political context within which policy-makers function. In each chapter, a brief orientation towards the educational system is also provided, as is a discussion of the relationship of LBP to the system's structure. Specific approaches to LBP are described, and are illustrated by examples of actual programmes. Each author concludes his chapter by addressing himself to the prospects for the continual development and growth of LBP. The final chapter draws together the major points contained in the study and attempts a systematic analysis of educational change in relation to Learning by Participation.

Notes and References

1. DEWEY. J. (1963). *Experience and Education*. New York: Collier.
2. RUST, V.D. (1977). *Alternatives in Education: Theoretical and Historical Perspectives*. London: Sage.
3. ABRAHAM, K. (1957). *Der Betrieb als Erziehungsfaktor*. Freiburg: Lambertus.
4. TOFFLER, A. (1970). *Future Shock*. New York: Bantam.
5. DEWEY, J. (1899). *School and Society*. Chicago: University of Chicago Press.
6. *Ibid.*

7. CREMIN, L.A. (1964). *The Transformation of the School.* New York: Vintage.
8. SILBERMAN, C. (1970). *Crisis in the Classroom.* New York: Random House.
9. GOODLAD, J.I. (1964). *School Curriculum Reform in the United States.* New York: Fund for the Advancement of Education.
10. DEWEY, J. (1961). *Democracy and Education.* New York: Macmillan.
11. NEILL, A.S. (1969). Summerhill: A Radical Approach to Child Rearing. New York: Hart.
12. ILLICH, I. (1971). *Deschooling Schooling.* London: Calder and Boyars.
13. LISTER, I. (1976). *Deschooling Revisited* (unpublished paper obtained from the University of York, England).
14. SILBERMAN, J. (1970). *op. cit.*
15. BROWN, F.B. (1973). *The Reform of Secondary Education.* National Commission on the Reform of Secondary Education. New York: McGraw-Hill.
16. REED, B. and BAZALGETTE, J. (1977). 'Education for Mature Responsibility'. An unpublished paper, written in the UK.
17. LISTER, I. (1976). *op. cit.*
18. REED, B. and BAZALGETTE, J. (1977). *op. cit.*
19. COLEMAN, J.S. (1974). Youth: Transition to Adulthood. Report of the President's Science Advisory Committee. Chicago: University of Chicago Press.
20. LISTER, I. (1976). *op. cit.*
21. ORGANIZATION FOR ECONOMIC CHANGE AND DEVELOPMENT (OECD). (1977). *Education and Working Life.* Paris: OECD.
22. BRISON, D.W. (1975). Peterborough Alternative Education Project. A Report to the Ministry of Education, Ontario. Toronto: Ontario Institute for Studies in Education.
23. MITCHELL, J.J. (1975). *The Adolescent Predicament.* Toronto: Holt, Rhinehart and Winston (Canada).
24. NORMAN, R. (1977). 'New Zealand's Community Volunteers Help Secondary Students to Meet Local Needs', *Synergist*, 6, 1 (Spring).
25. SILBERMAN, H. (1975). 'Involving the Young', *Phi Delta Kappan.* 56, 596-600.
26. DICKSON, A. (1973). Keynote address, National Conference for Directors and Advisers of Student Volunteer Programmes, National Student Volunteer Program ACTION, Chigaco, 1st October 1973.
27. CAEL (1975). *Assessing Prior Learning – A CAEL Student Guide.* A manual prepared by Aubrey Forrest for Cooperative Assessment of Experiential Learning.
28. COLEMAN, J.S. (1972). 'Children Have Outgrown the Schools', *Phi Delta Kappan*, 54, 226-30.
29. SCRIBNER, J. and COLE, M. (1973). *Culture and Thought*, New York: John Wiley.
30. MORRIS and KEETON (Ed) (1976). In COLEMAN, J.S. *Differences Between Experiential and Classroom Learning.* (Chapter Five). San

Francisco: Jossey-Bass.
31. WOODS, D.E. (1977). 'What Next? An International Perspective on the Future of Service Programs for Secondary Students', *Synergist*, 6, 1 (Spring).
32. COOMBS, P.H. and AHMED, M. (1974). *Attacking Rural Poverty: How Non-formal Education Can Help*. Baltimore: John Hopkins University Press.

CHAPTER TWO

The Netherlands

LEENDERT VAN DEN BOSCH

The Netherlands may be the only country to have established a Ministerial-level commission devoted full-time to introducing Learning by Participation into the national upper secondary education system. The Innovatie Commissie Participatie-Onderwijs (ICP) or the Innovation Committee for Learning by Participation is working to change both educational practice, in accordance with LBP theory, and the structure of the Dutch educational system, with the goal that eventually every young person in the 16-19 age group can take part in LBP programmes. Leendert van den Bosch was a member of IPC and was its Acting Chairman from 1979-80.

Martha, a 16-year-old, is a student at a school in Amsterdam which has begun to implement Learning by Participation. She wants to pursue vocational education, but she does not really know what she wants to do nor, indeed, what she is able to do. She feels that her involvement with LBP has been helpful to her, as the comments she made to me during a conversation I had with her in 1978 show:

Over the next couple of days I'll be looking at a beauty parlour. I want to stay there for a while and try some of the jobs. I might like to become a beautician . . . I used to think that a job working with children would be nice, but after I'd tried working at a day nursery I realised it was not for me! Though when I talked it over with my group and with the teacher I realised it had been a good experience and had taught me a lot about myself. It helped me realise I don't enjoy working with children. So now I'd like to try a beauty parlour.

Discussion and post-experience analysis form an essential part of the process.

With three other girls interested in that type of work I read the information they had at school then we discussed it with a teacher. Now we've written a long list of questions we want to ask the staff, the boss and the clients of the beauty parlour, and when I've done that, and had my two days' experience, I'll have to write a report at school about it for my group of fifteen students to discuss.

Martha particularly appreciates the control she is able to exercise over her own school activities:

I am glad I am in this school – it is very free. Although I have to discuss my plans with a teacher and other students, the only person who decides what I shall do is me. In Social Orientation, for example, I've chosen to join the group studying drug addiction, and the teacher and I have drawn up my study-plan together. I've been coming to this school regularly every two months for half a year now – it's OK. Very different from my previous school. There it used to be very dull, but here I'm the one who decides what I want to learn. Now I sometimes even enjoy reading books because I can see the things that they are about in real life. In Social Orientation we don't only read and talk about drug addicts – we discuss our experiences and have interviews with them, and with social workers, doctors, police officers and so on. We are making a report and perhaps a video tape about the facts and our conclusions, and we are going to try getting a newspaper interested in it. I'm never bored. And I'm still learning a great deal.

(Taken from a conversation between the author and a student in 1978.)

In the Netherlands, Learning by Participation is a topic which plays an important role in discussion of the future of young people aged from 16 to 18 or 19. There is a generally felt need for educational reform at the upper secondary level, and national decision-makers see Learning By Participation as the leading principle for such reform.

Unions, parent organizations, national school organizations, organizations of employers, politicians, scientists and so on are in agreement with the ideas expressed by Dollar and Rust in Chapter

One that secondary education has become too much a closed system with its own structures and processes; that a gap has opened between the school and the society and between the school and the individual student.

Dissatisfaction is expressed among young people, with what are seen as irrelevant school curricula, the dominance of standards and values associated with a middle-class sub-culture and the subject-oriented form into which schools distil the educational process. From a national sample taken in 1976, which questioned 16–17-year-olds on their attitudes to school, more than 60 per cent were negative. More and more, there is a growing awareness that these negative attitudes stem from more than 'merely' problems of motivation, and that a solution requires something other than dull ways of teaching. We must look for ways to restore the relationship between the school and the social systems outside it.

Motives for Support of Learning by Participation

The groups in the Netherlands which support the Learning By Participation movement have differing motives for their support. Six categories of motives may be distinguished:

a. the expectations of many people that Learning By Participation will have an appeal for the early school-leavers, who, especially at a time of rapidly increasing unemployment, are socially vulnerable;

b. the posibility that Learning By Participation may be an approach through which young 'drop-outs' – registered as students but for whom, because of absenteeism and behaviour problems, school has no meaning – can develop their abilities;

c. that Learning By Participation may help young people to gain better insight into the relations between social reality and their own needs;

d. the belief that Learning By Participation will enable both school and student to gather more up-to-date knowledge about the world of work, and thereby increase the students' chances of making successful career choices;

e. the feeling, referred to many times in this study, that adolescents are an under-utilized resource, held outside society, and made to feel meaningless within it;

f. the complaint that young people receive theoretical knowledge, but do not learn to solve concrete problems in a social situation. The LBP approach, relating theoretical knowledge to work in the solution of real problems, is thus supported by many.

Two approaches

The motives outlined above point to two possible approaches to the implementation of LBP. In one of them, Learning By Participation is seen as a new possibility for achieving the ideal of equal opportunities, which was the dream of Dutch educational politics in the 1960s – every boy and girl must have the same chance for a career, regardless of his or her social background.

Not until the 1970s did it become clear that traditional education cannot make up for differences in the social backgrounds of the students; now it is hoped that LBP will help young people from the lower social classes, in particular, to achieve better educational results. A danger here, suggested by Noel Kershaw in Chapter Three, is that LBP will become associated with second-rate education.

The second approach sees LBP as an answer to the crisis in secondary education, outlined by Dollar and Rust in their summary of the criticism of the 'deschooling movement' (Chapter one, pp. 15-17). LBP seeks to restore the link between in- and out-of school learning, to restore the school's service function as a place where people who want to, can learn. And importantly, it rejects the function of the school as a place where young people should be controlled. As an alternative school concept, it is hoped that it offers better possibilities to young people of the working classes.

Political Background

The history of LBP in the Netherlands is a long one, dominated in its early years by the first of these approaches. In attempts to facilitate the expansion of compulsory education from the age of fourteen to eighteen years the Government promoted and sponsored programmes following LBP principles – this was, in part, a response to demands and demonstrations in 1969.

In more recent years the second approach has taken stronger hold and secondary education reform has meant, among other things, that compulsory education now stops at sixteen. This has eradicated the direct link between LBP and compulsory education, and has altered the balance of LBP support so that support from the trade unions and the labour party has decreased while that within the education system and from the employers' organizations has increased. While the teachers see it as a goal in itself for young people to be regarded as students rather than as unemployed, they frankly recognize the existence of problems that they face daily in the classroom, problems of students who 'do not want to learn' and who continually criticize the school. More and more, teachers are becoming open to alternative approaches which may help to solve their problems.

In addition to the initiatives of policy-makers, a small increase of innovation initiatives has taken place at the school level, as far as this is possible in a highly centralized system. It should be appreciated that such innovation is difficult to carry out, demanding as it does strong motivation to deviate from ordinary practice and to use the meshes of a bureaucratic system; the usual attitude of schools and teachers to the solution of general problems is to wait for guidelines from the central decision-level.

It is also relevant for the Learning By Participation movement that the concept has been introduced into the educational politics of the European Community. The ministers of education of the nine countries have taken the decision to sponsor model programmes, which are directed at a better transition from school to the world of work. With regard to implementation of this decision, the need for an educational concept was felt, which led to a discussion of this problem and the introduction of the idea of LBP.

In the Netherlands many interest-groups and organizations are involved in the definition and implementation of Learning by Participation. The contrasts in interests result, naturally, in different definitions. Indeed, the Learning by Participation concept is used sometimes as a panacea for all kinds of problems: a danger is that Learning by Participation might become a 'container-concept' where the meaning and implementation of the concept is affected by political compromises. These compromises are sometimes not only impossible to implement in practice but can even be inconsistent with the concept.

An example of this is provided by the negotiations at the central decision level concerning internships. An 'internship' means that students work as part of the educational programme in a factory or social agency to learn certain insights and skills. Schools make arrangements with factories and social agencies about the learning-goals, the activities of the student and the organization of the internship. The length of an internship varies, and depends on the learning goals and learning possibilities in each concrete situation. Trade unions, fearing exploitation of students as cheap employees, demand payment of the student by the employer. For their part, the employers demand financial compensation, because they invest time in the cooperation with schools. During the negotiations one proposed compromise was to replace internships by simulations in school. However, in the Learning by Participation concept simula-tions can never replace real participation in practical situations out of school, although simulations can be used for preparation and/or evaluation of real participation. Learning by Participation is more than application of theoretical knowledge. The participation of students in activities which are useful both for society and for the development of the student is essential.

Such an example is typical of a centralized educational system, where the implementation of ideas in school practice is a political issue as well. The Dutch educational system is centralized and a reflection of a society with dividing lines between several social classes.

At this point, a definition of Learning by Participation as the term is understood in the Netherlands would be appropriate. Later in this chapter the definition will be expanded in connection with a discussion of the central role played by the Innovation Committee for Learning By Participation (ICP).

A Definition of Learning by Participation

Learning By Participation, as the Dutch see it, aims at providing young people with the skills they need to solve problems in practical situations, to think independently, and to participate effectively in a social context. It involves broadening the traditional concept of learning by incorporating both the community and the school in their entirety as possible resources for the curriculum and by involving young people as responsible citizens in real-life situations as a basis for learning. In Chapter One Dollar and Rust stress that the major principles of LBP are participation in society, critical reflection on that participation, and the relating of experience to theoretical knowledge, all of which are in some degree controlled by the student who takes part in decision-making.

Ways in which these principles are put into practice will of course vary according to each country's temperament and existing social and educational systems. The Netherlands stresses the *integration of a broad set of learning goals*, derived from the requirements an individual must meet in a practical situation. Student programmes designed to incorporate LBP principles include a *wider range of out-of-school experiences which provide participation in society*, and the student aims *to develop greater independence in decision-making, problem-solving and planning*. 'Critical reflection' becomes a constant part of the LBP process.

The following two brief cases will illustrate the way these principles can be put into practice in Holland.

Case one: In 1973 the principal of a school in Amsterdam[1] read a report about Learning by Participation. The report contained ideas which he had already been thinking about for years. He talked about the report with some teachers and members of the school board. They formed a small working group and worked for some months on a plan for a programme, based on Learning by Participation. They sent the plan to the Ministry of Education, and were invited several times to talk with civil servants about their plan. After some hesitation they agreed, subject to certain conditions, to found a new school for the programme and that the number of students would be limited to 100 for the time being. In 1975 they received both permission and money to begin. Preparation was more difficult than they had thought it would be, but in 1976 the new school opened with 100 students.

The target group of the programme is young people, 16- and 17-year-olds, who have had little success in their school careers. Most of them are either school drop-outs, or do not meet the requirements of any formal qualification. The programme pursues learning goals of three kinds: goals pertaining to skills for acting in social situations;

goals relating to obtaining a diploma or entering further (mostly vocational) education; and career education goals, such as orientation to the world of work, skills for entering the work force, and skills for a certain trade or profession.

The programme starts with an orientation period of four weeks, during which the student is trained in the working methods of the programme. A lot of attention is given to the emotional effects on each student of his or her past personal experience in the school system. As part of their orientation, students in small groups visit a variety of sites in the world of work, where they observe and talk to as many people as possible. These experiences are then discussed and 'processed', using non-verbal methods, and teachers take part in giving guidance to new students.

After the orientation period, the programme offers three types of activities. First there are activities in which all students must participate, which include courses in basic skills such as reading and writing, creative expression, sport and the so-called social orientation. The course in social orientation is developed from key problems which students encounter in situations outside the school. As part of this course, students have assignments to gather information from resources outside the school, including people, agencies, institutions, factories and so forth.

The second type of programme activity consists of optional courses, which usually last two months. A student, having made a choice for a certain trade or for a certain school for further education, will use the time for optional courses to follow a course that will qualify him or her for that job or that school. The optional courses are specifically tailored to the individual needs of each student.

Internships are the third type of programme activity, in which students spend one or two days a week in a factory or social agency. The maximum length of an internship in one organization is eight weeks. The student is expected to do work during the internship, but the work activities are derived from learning-goals to ensure that they have educational or developmental value. In addition, the student gathers information during the internship experience that may be used back at the school. This is based on the training the student received at school in the techniques of data collecting.

At the work site one adult is responsible for the guidance of the student, having been trained for the task at a workshop conducted at the school. Each teacher at the school has a group of 15 students with whom the teacher meets, both in individual and group sessions. One teacher, who is called the Internship Coordinator, is responsible for the recruitment of internship sites, an analysis of the learning possibilities at these sites, arrangements with the agencies and factories, and so forth. The Internship Coordinator, in other words, organizes the learning situations outside the school.

In spite of many difficulties the programme is considered a success. Every year more than a hundred young people who have given up the regular school system try to join the programme. Part of the original plan was to disseminate the programme to other schools in Amsterdam after a certain period, but so far this has not happened; one reason is that most schools prefer to assign 'difficult students' to some other school rather than to implement a special programme of their own for them. Another reason is that the staff of the programme have not made a detailed description of it. Their feeling is that the programme is still in the development stage, and that, additionally, every year improvements are made and the staff members do not find the time for dissemination activities. In the meantime, the school has also some vocational programmes besides the above-mentioned orientation programme.

Case two: A school in another city, Hengelo, introduced a three-month programme[2] in 1976 for 16- and 17-year-olds who were uncertain and aimless about their future plans. The programme helps these directionless students to begin taking responsibility for their own future and to make realistic decisions. It helps students to overcome psychological blocks caused by previous school experience, and to discover that there are alternative ways to learn. The main objectives of the programme for students are to learn how to make career decisions, and it is expected that every student who completes the programme will recognise the importance of, and will develop, basic skills, since these are important for the career goals of every young person.

The programme begins with an intensive intake process, after which the students work as a group for a week somewhere in the country. The focus during this week is on relationships and contacts within the group. For the rest of the programme the central feature is a specially developed model or method for problem solving, as shown in Table 1.

Table 1

1	2	3	4	5	6
What is the question? What is now exactly the problem?	Which *aspects* have this problem? *Key-words.*	What *exactly* do I want to know?	Gathering of the necessary *information* (where, how, by whom) by: – asking – observing – reading – participating + *processing.*	*judging* information. Which data are worthwhile *for me?*	judgement or *decision* and how will it continue?

The problem-solving model is employed in four areas of programme activity, as follows:

School: (first encounter with the problem-solving method): the method is applied to former and current school experiences;

Work: students apply the method, with guidance, to the world of work; this phase includes an orientation to the world of work and a preliminary evaluation of career wishes;

Internship: students now apply the method independently in a practical situation outside the school;

Career expectation: students apply the model to their own career goals.

Most of the activities in the School, Work and Career Expectation projects take place at the school. Out-of-school activities related to these consist of short visits to factories and social agencies for observation and interviewing. In the internship project, however, every student works one day for training in techniques for gathering information, while the other day is for processing the information and sharing experiences. The activities of the student at the internship sites are intensively evaluated.

Besides the four projects, each student receives intensive individual counselling. The students also attend courses in mathematics, social science, Dutch and English. All these courses are related to concrete problems and situations which the students meet in the world outside the school.

These two short case impressions illustrate three characteristics of the Learning by Participation movement in the Netherlands. First, the main target group of the programmes are the 'problem students', the educationally disadvantaged. This was a systematic policy of the national Ministry of Education which gives permission and money only for programmes with this target group. This focus of the central decision level is now changing. From 1979, the national ministry has also sponsored Learning by Participation programmes for schools considered to be of a higher level.

A second characteristic is the strong centralization of the Dutch educational system. All schools in secondary education are wholly maintained financially by the national Ministry of Education.

A third characteristic is the concentration of the Learning by Participation movement on upper secondary education.

The present Dutch educational system

Efforts to introduce Learning by Participation in the Netherlands have concentrated on innovations at the upper secondary level; that is, on students between the ages of 16 and 19. In the national policy, Learning by Participation is one part of a broad plan to introduce reforms into every level of the educational system.[4]

It will take time and understanding successfully to achieve the changes in structure and practice that this plan envisions. Recognizing this, the government appointed commissions to give advice on innovations at all levels of the system. One commission is briefed to offer advice, and to initiate and to support innovative programmes that will result in the implementation of Learning by Participation at upper secondary level. The situation of this commission, the Innovation Committee for Learning by Particiaption (I.C.P.) in relation to the rest of the system is illustrated in Figure 2.

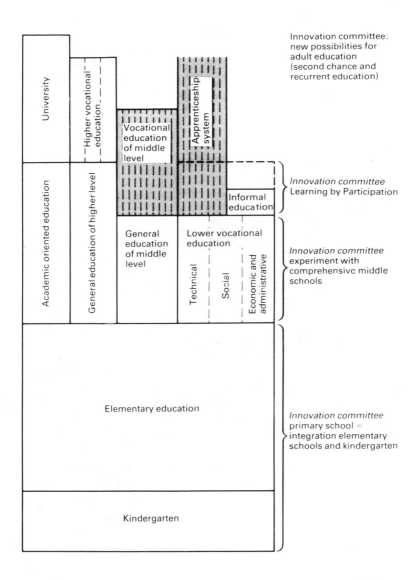

Figure 2

A brief description of the current educational system and the proposed changes will be helpful.

Under the present system, Dutch children start schooling when they enter kindergarten at the age of four. After two years they enter the elementary school. The government wants to integrate the kindergarten and the elementary school to form a new school to be called 'Basisschool' or primary school. An innovation committee guides this process and advises the Education Minister about progress in reaching this goal.

After elementary school, as shown in Figure 2, the child is confronted with a very divided system. There the selection process starts. Every child is labelled, and that has a decisive influence on his or her future. The maximum level of education attainable for many chldren is determined at the age of 12. Since there is a strong correllation between a pupil's social class background and that pupil's later success in school, it is not surprising that only three per cent of university students are from the lower social class. A part of the government's reform plan is intended to rectify this imbalance.

In 1973, an innovation committee was established to prepare the introduction of a comprehensive middle school that will eventually replace the current highly divided system. There are now some experimental middle schools in development.

Under the present system, students of the lower vocational schools leave these schools at the age of 16. These students constitute about 40 per cent of any total age group. They can choose between informal education and the apprenticeship system, with a very small number able to go on to (middle level) vocational education. 20 to 25 per cent of this group, however, do not obtain a diploma and so are not accepted by the apprenticeship system.

Furthermore, a condition for part-time vocational training in the apprenticeship system is that the student should have a job. However, in recent years, unemployment in the Netherlands has become more common for school leavers than having a job. The only further education prospect possible for these young people is to attend schools which provide informal general education. As long as the young person has not reached his or her seventeenth birthday, attendance at the schools is compulsory for two days a week. Unfortunately, these schools do nothing directly to help their students enter the labour market. The programmes are directed exclusively at personal growth and social skills, and do not offer any formal certificate upon completion. For these reasons informal education has a reputation for being a 'dead end road'.

Students who complete the middle-level general education schools can go on to the middle-level vocational schools, and, in some cases, to the last two grades of higher-level general education schools. But access to these schools is limited to students who are very successful and who obtain a diploma. Yet 30 per cent leave these middle-level vocational schools without a diploma. These students are allowed to pursue a diploma in a lower vocational school or can try to be accepted by the small number of linking possibilities that lead to middle vocational education. Or they may try to find a job, which sometimes can be combined with a course in the apprenticeship system.

As for the position of students in the academic schools and in higher-level general education, Figure 2 provides a clear enough picture for the purposes of this discussion.

The Innovation Committee for Learning by Participation (I.C.P.) is charged with innovation of education at the upper secondary level. In general terms, the I.C.P. seeks to make two kinds of change. First, it seeks to change educational practice in general in accordance with the principles and objectives of learning by participation. Second, the I.C.P. seeks to change the structure of the educational system in such a way as to allow every young person aged 16–19 the opportunity to participate in meaningful educational programmes of which the goals, subjects, methods and perspectives are in accordance witth students' needs and abilities. The I.C.P. has pursued these two goals by publishing a series of reports and initiating numerous activities.

When the I.C.P. was initiated, the Dutch government gave greater emphasis to the second goal, calling for changes in the educational structure. The I.C.P., on the other hand, has emphasized the first goal, relating to changes in educational practice by implementing Learning by Participation. Gradually the government has adjusted its policy to accord with the opinions of the I.C.P. Changes in the administrative structure of the system can be carried out with no necessary effect on actual school practice.

The position taken by the I.C.P. derives from a belief that ordinary practice in many schools has such severe shortcomings that structural changes will not solve their problems. School practice in itself serves as a blockade for many young people. Only changes in school practice can remove these blockades. National policy can do no more than stimulate and support these changes.

Innovation in a centralized system

The description above shows the centralized character of the decision-making process. At secondary level every school is 100 per cent financially dependent on the national Ministry. Every school, for example, must follow the central guidelines for the number of students per teacher and the number of hours for every subject discipline. The national Ministry decides which courses are mandatory for every student and what kind of optional courses a school can offer; whether most courses should finish with a national examination and so forth. A local schoolboard has little power. When there are enough students a board can appoint a teacher – that is to say, the board can choose from among those applicants who meet the nationally determined requirements.

Reform of the Dutch education system is greatly complicated by a tripartite vertical division of the schools. At every level there are three separate schools: a Protestant school, a Roman Catholic school and a non-denominational school. Every school has its own board, which manages the school within the narrow margins of the central guidelines.

At the national level there are national organizations of schoolboards and teacher unions. These national organisations negotiate with each other and with the government about the central guidelines. They have a strong impact on the decision-making process.

In such a situation there is little room for spontaneous grass-roots innovation. If teachers and schoolboards want essential changes in educational practice they must start with action outside the school. They must obtain sufficient support for their wishes to be discussed around the national negotiation table. A positive outcome in such cases means mostly that the central level allows some deviations from the usual guidelines. In order to use these opportunities to deviate, a school must send a request to the national department of education, and such a request must be strongly motivated. It takes at least several months, and in some cases several years, before the buraucracy produces a decision about the request. Innovative teachers must have strong motivation, a lot of perseverance, some political skills and relationships with key persons. An innovation effort that starts at central level, with fewer relationships with actual activities in schools, has its own problems: a disproportionately large investment of manpower in conceptualization and in national decision-making is made at the cost of little implementation of the innovation in practice, and a difficult accommodation of local situations or national interest. National innovations carry a danger of producing hollow results. New words are used for a practice which has not really changed. Reports tell of results which cannot be observed in actual practice.

Fortunately, an awareness has grown that the centralized structure of the system is also a problem in the realization of centrally-promoted innovations. In addition, the influence of those persons involved in innovative work is also growing. There is a tendency to combine innovative actions at the central level with actual movements in schools. Networks of persons who work at different levels of the system are being formed. This is probably the best innovation strategy for the Dutch situation: combinations of action at the central level and the school level. It is essential for the implementation of Learning by Participation that teachers and students gain more responsibility over school practice. Their creativity must be challenged. They must have the opportunity to develop and to implement their own ideas.

Learning by Participation at the central level: 3 plans[5]

The Innovation Committee for Learning by Participation (I.C.P.) has designed programmes to influence national policy on education at the upper secondary level, school practice and the work of R&D centres. At the request of the government, the I.C.P. developed three plans for innovation at the upper secondary level. As depicted in Figure 3, plan I applies to the lower-level schools, plan II to the middle-level schools and plan III to the academic and higher-level schools.

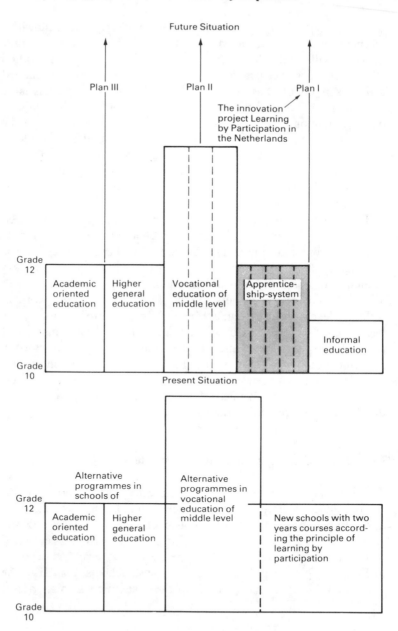

Figure 3

Plan I, which calls for new two-year programmes to be developed by the schools for informal education and the organizations of the apprenticeship system cooperatively, incorporates principles of LBP and changes the present situation in several ways. Firstly, it enables all students between the ages of 16 and 19 to undertake full-time study leading to qualification either for a job or for further education. Secondly, it concentrates attention on the development of personal and social identities and skills and, lastly, it adopts as its educational approach the combination of out-of-school practical experiences as a part of the curriculum with in-school learning activities. The key structural aim of the plan is to replace informal education and the first two years of the apprenticeship system with schools offering the new programme.

Much activity has resulted. In the framework of plan I, seven so-called experimental schools were given the opportunity to implement the Learning by Participation concept in all their curricula; funds have been granted for more experimental schools, and other schools implement Learning by Participation in some part of their curricula. (The two examples given earlier in this chapter are programmes which come within the framework of plan I.) The majority of those schools which are connected with the apprenticeship system in connection with the schools for informal education are preparing plans for alternative programmes based on Learning by Participation. A wide range of what are called 'stimulating activities', coordinated by a group of specialists, has taken place at national and local level: examples include exchanges of teachers between schools, demonstrations, information brochures and how-to-do-it guides. Some provision has been made for evaluation, but an overall plan is still in preparation – there is a shortage of qualified people for systematic evaluation. Broader and more intensive involvement in school practice is not easy as bureaucratic procedures act as a barrier.

Plan II aims to generate experiments in which middle vocational education is organized in accordance with LBP principles, and to encourage cooperation between these experiments and the new schools created under plan I. Young people from the 'lower classes' will thus have the opportunity to obtain qualifications for higher level jobs, and to attain a higher general level of professional competency. A long-term goal, if plan II produces positive results, will be the eventual integration of middle vocational schools and the new schools of plan I.

The implementation of plan II is strongly influenced by the governmental decision, made apparently in order to reduce youth unemployment figures, to keep young people who are usually not accepted by middle vocational schools in the school system longer. Additional funding is made available to schools if they develop special programmes for these young people, but although the government requires the Learning by Participation concept to be implemented in the new programmes, this is seldom checked, and the most important thing seems to be that boys and girls who would otherwise be registered as unemployed are now registered as students.

Plan III has two short-term goals. First, it aims to establish more familiarity with and good will towards the idea of Learning by Participation among schools, organizations and decision makers that are involved in the academic oriented and higher general education part of upper secondary education. The second immediate goal is to develop and implement experimental programmes of Learning by Participation at demonstration sites at the higher education level.

The government has expressed support for the goals of plan III, but up to now the priority of this plan within the policy of the government is unclear. Little money has been granted.

Before giving more information about the I.C.P's strategy for the realisation of the three plans, we describe first the definition of Learning by Participation as it is used in the plans.

The definition of Learning by Participation at the central level[6]

The concept of Learning by Participation as used at the central level in the Netherlands has three main characteristics:

integration of a broad set of learning goals;
individualization of the learning process;
a combination of theory application and action within and out of the school.

The learning goals are not derived from independent subject disciplines, but rather from the requirements an individual must meet in a practical situation. An example of the former approach would be to start with the question, 'What must a student know and be able to do concerning mathematics?' The answer would involve breaking down mathematics into components to be learned by the student. In the latter approach the pertinent question is: 'What does a student need in order to work effectively toward solving problems posed by concrete situations?'

The following categories of skills can be employed for the formulating of learning goals and the analysis of practical situations:

Technical-instrumental skills: Skills to perform a task in a professional manner. Examples: proper use of an instrument, machine or tool; report making; letter writing;

Communication skills: Skills in working and cooperating with others. Examples: listening, handling social conventions, participating in group discussions, playing and enjoying together;

Political skills: Skills related to the existing labour and power structure, involving knowledge and understanding of social processes. Examples: political decision making, roles of men and women, roles of trade unions, personal career perspectives;

Value skills: Skills to clarify and express values in concrete situations as a means of developing personal identitiy. Examples: awareness in personal relations with others, anticipation of personal conflicts, forming political opinions;

Change skills: Skills to change both situations and oneself. Examples: negotiating, experimenting, changing of habits, becoming an active member of an organization, taking initiative, etc.

All of these skills are integrated into the learning programme of every student.

In addition, three types of learning activities are combined in each student's programme: out-of-school activities, personal and social guidance and instruction. In the out-of-school component, one can distinguish the following kinds of activities:

1. Action projects that make some positive contribution to the community, such as services for old people, action research on environmental issues, restoration of old buildings. Project work is undertaken by the students themselves, who are given a maximum of responsibility;

2. Observation and orientation, which takes place in practical situations and may be long or short-term. Short-term orientations are intended to orient students to different kinds of out-of-school situations in order to help them make a choice as to which one to participate in most intensively. A longer term observation would place a student in a 'shadow learning' situation, in which the student follows an adult in his or her workplace to learn about that type of work;
3. Internship: this means that the student works for a certain period in a factory or social agency. The student's activity is derived from specific learning goals which have been formulated jointly in discussion among student, school and the 'employer'.

Most schools use combinations of the three types of out-of-school activities.

It is important that the school makes very explicit arrangements in advance about the content and character of the activities. Thus, a key condition is a thorough analysis of the learning resources offered by potential out-of-school sites. The *guidance phase* of Learning By Participation serves to facilitate the connection between the learning process and the needs, interests and capabilities of the student. This connection is a reciprocal one: not only does the guidance result in the formulation, realization, evaluation and eventually correction of the learning plan of each student, but also the guidance results in modifications in the content of the learning programme based on what is discovered about the student's needs. In addition since learning to assure responsibility for one's own development is a central feature of Learning by Participation, this is a major focus of the guidance portion of the programme.

While Learning by Participation attempts to realize as much of the learning process as possible through concrete experience in practical situations, there is still a need for course work inside the schools. This applies to the learning of basic skills in particular. A variety of methods may be used in the institution phase of the programme, including lectures, individualized learning packages, tutorials, workshops, and so forth. Learning by Participation in the Netherlands is individualized in the sense that a personal learning plan is formulated for each student. This occurs, in conjunction with individual guidance, immediately after an orientation period at the beginning of the programme. Important data for this learning plan include the history of the student as well as his or her career goals, capabilities, and other needs, and also requirements of further education and learning resources both within and out of the school. The plan describes activities for the student in all three components: out-of-school, guidance, and institutional. A number of standards of objectives has been set for use as a guide in formulating the plan, as in the following examples:

the student must become aware of his or her own situation, and of possibilities for changing this situation;
learning activities must show a gradual increase in variety, complexity and opportunities for taking responsibility;
the learning plan must bring the student to greater independence in decision making, in problem solving and in planning his or her own learning process;
the learning plan must connect the learning activities with the actual situation and present needs of the student;
the learning plan must make it possible for the student either to take part in further education or to apply for a job.

Learning by Participation requires a redefinition of the traditional role of the teacher. The teacher is no longer exclusively an instructor, although that remains a part of the role, but must adapt to the emphasis on guidance. The new role may be described as a learning guide or learning coordinator or learning facilitator. It entails the guidance of students, both as groups and as individuals, in planning their own learning processes, while providing professional resources and adult support. A demand made by this role which may be entirely new to some teachers is to identify and make contact with learning resources outside the school. In schools that have implemented Learning by Participation, one or more staff persons may be assigned to the acquisition, classification, analysis and coordination of these resources.

Strategies at central level

For the design of innovation strategies an analysis of the position of the initiator is very important. Every position has its advantages and disadvantages. The principal of a school who takes the initiative for an innovation has an advantage in his direct relationship with the practising teachers. But it is difficult for him or her to bring about the necessary decisions at central level. A national commission has more ability to influence the central decision-level, but the danger is that school practice will not really change. We speak in this context about 'paper innovations'. Many people are involved, write reports, have meetings and conferences, guidelines are carefully formulated, implementation plans are financed, but a student notices almost no change in practice. People can write excellent things when they get money for it. The Innovation Committee Learning by Participation (I.C.P.) does not think Learning by Participation can be implemented on a large scale only by influencing the decision process at national level. This influence is necessary in a centralized system, but not sufficiently for real implementation. Besides, it is essential for the implementation of Learning by Participation that schools and teachers become less dependent on central guidelines in the development of programmes. To convince central decision-makers of the need for innovative educational practice may be difficult, but to convince central decision-makers to delegate responsibility to the teacher is much more so. Central decision-makers accept that they can fail, although they speak in such cases about evaluation and the necessity of improvements. But teachers must also have the opportunity and the right to fail.

The function which the I.C.P. performs in the implementation process has similarities with the function of a teacher as a learning facilitator in a Learning by Participation programme at school level. This teacher organizes a learning climate for his students both in and out of the school. The I.C.P. tries to organize a climate for innovation at the central level and the school level. The committee builds up relationships with institutes and persons at all levels in order to facilitate the acceptance, implementation and dissemination of Learning by Participation. In this way networks of relations are built up with schools, individual teachers, policy makers, interest groups, R and D centres, journalists, civil servants, and so forth. The methods used depend on the target group and the stage of the innovation process. The I.C.P. speaks of a stimulating or activating strategy, a development strategy and an evaluation strategy.

The *stimulating or activating strategy*, aimed chiefly at teachers, school leaders and community members, is designed to induce these people to think about how Learning by Participation may be implemented in their own local settings. Reports on exemplary programmes and conferences with teachers about these reports are examples of activities within the stimulating strategy.[7]

As a part of the stimulating strategy, the I.C.P. published a book with a framework for the development of Learning by Participation programmes at school level and extended descriptions and analysis of some programmes.[8] A number of conferences are organized where teachers discuss the book and the implementation possibilities in their own schools. Another activity within the stimulation strategy is visits of teams of three persons to programmes in other countries.[9] The participants were helped by discussing their experiences with colleagues. Meetings are also arranged between teachers and policy makers. Teachers tell about their programmes at conferences and so forth.

The *development strategy* involves the creation of conditions for the development and implementation of alternative programmes. Examples of such activities include developing models for Learning by Participation programmes, inservice training of teachers, support for consultants and other expert resources, extra development money, legal arrangements, and so forth.[10] Part of the development strategy includes activities to identify movements at the local level which can be related to the implementation of the Learning by Participation concept. In such cases the I.C.P. builds up a relationship and gives publicity to such an initiative. The conceptual framework of the I.C.P. and the local ideas are integrated to plan the innovation process in such a local situation.

In a school for middle vocational education, for example, a four-year programme in mechanical engineering for 16 students was based largely on the construction and installation of an astronomical observatory in a local museum. Another vocational school in the field of agriculture developed a programme in which students aged 16, 17 and 18 take on the entire responsibility of a farm for one year.

In an academic-oriented school, a teacher in economics based his course on a consumer-action programme. The students investigated differences in prices and the causes for these differences, and they published accounts of their work in local newspapers.

These relationships between the central Learning by Participation concept and local programmes not only facilitate the visibility of the concept, but also lead to the continuation and extension of local programmes. Experience has shown that a local initiative usually has a short life if it does not get external support.

Another aspect of the development strategy is to form relationships with other national innovation projects. An example of a project is the reorganization of vocational education for jobs in welfare services. The plan is to integrate twenty different fields of study into nine. The I.C.P. gives suggestions on how the Learning by Participation concept can be implemented in new curricula.

Another part of the development strategy is to give help to teachers and schools who want to implement Learning by Participation but do not know how to do it. The help can be extra money for staff, the design of a programme model or arrangements for information exchanges between schools.

The *evaluation strategy* entails initiating a capability for delineating, obtaining and providing useful information about the process, results and other effects of the innovation, and about procedures for taking decisions based on this information. Features of this evaluation strategy include, for example, a group of researchers which reports on the experimental schools, the development of questionnaires and other evaluation instruments, the yearly determination of priorities for applying for new experiments, and so on.

The evaluation strategy is a weak link in the work of the I.C.P. This is partly a matter of priority. In the present stage of the Learning by Participation movement it is more important to create a positive climate and a large number of examples of Learning by Participation on school level. On the other hand, strongly motivated innovators have a tendency to neglect systematic evaluation. In the long term this can become a danger. Another factor is the lack of expertise for evaluation of a very complicated innovation process.

Illustrations of barriers and change forces

Implementation of Learning by Participation in school practice has far-reaching consequences for the organization of the school and the school's external relationships, in whichever country it may be introduced. Many of the barriers to implementation existing in the Netherlands mirror those to be found in Scandinavia, the UK or the US, and to a greater or lesser degree implementation of LBP will also affect a number of persons and institutions that are not directly involved in the teaching-learning process. This is espcially true in the Dutch situation.

Though it is difficult, it makes sense to distinguish between barriers and resistance. Barriers are problems which in principle can be solved. Resistance has to do with the rejection of an innovation for ideological reasons. Very often barriers are expressed as resistance. For example, a group of teachers formulated political objections against Learning by Participation. This innovation, they felt, would reduce the pedagogic task of the school, because there are fewer contacts between the teacher and his students. It appeared that the teachers in fact feared a reduction of the social importance of teachers. This barrier can be removed by spreading information about the teacher's role in Learning by Participation programmes.

However, another group of so-called critical teachers rejects the goals of Learning by Participation. They believe the school should not have many linkages with social reality. Rejecting the present society, they want to teach their students, in the protected situation of the school, to analyse society and to prepare them for an alternative to the present social situations. They see the school as a sheltered breeding ground for an alternative society. In this case one can speak of resistance to Learning by Participation. The statements of the new group do not have much direct influence on the implementation process, but indirectly they do. Their criticism is used by others who fear a threat to their own interests in Learning by Participation.

Implementation problems and barriers are interrelated, and thus responses to them must always take their complexity into account. Very often innovators do not have the resources to take desirable action.

Barriers are essential in an innovation process. They force the innovator to evaluate and to improve the innovation; they prevent innovation for innovation's sake. Many barriers point out the shortcomings of the innovation process. Insight into the barriers, then, must be combined with insight into the forces of change. Who loses and who wins by the innovation?

The six motives for support mentioned at the beginning of this chapter are important forces for change, but they could become barriers if Learning by Participation failed to meet a specific expectation. A number of administrators, for example, are in favour of Learning by Participation because they expect a reduction in the number of school leavers without a diploma; so it is important to give publicity to the result that a high percentage of students successfully finish their participation in a Learning by Participation programme.

An incentive for many teachers is that their relationships with students improve through Learning by Participation. They get more social and emotional affirmation from the students. In fact the students are the most important supporters of the Learning by Participation movement, and it would make sense to organize this support. In all evaluation reports students are very positive. This helps teachers to overcome their own psychological barriers.

Teachers read and hear many negative remarks about the school system. This creates uncertainty and demoralizes them. Learning by Participation seems to improve the image of the school.

For young teachers, especially, reduction of the rigidity of the organization of the school is a change force to be viewed with favour. The teacher's situation is more flexible, and he has a greater posibility of following his own interpretation of the job. However, this same feature can be a barrier for other teachers. A strong parental incentive to support LBP is that the programmes offer drop-outs new chances.

The question of a public image, or the image of an agency, can sometimes provide an incentive. Some administrators, for example, are very eager for the publicity which accompanies an I.C.P. report; but others are happy with the publicity that comes from criticizing the work of the I.C.P.

There are a number of barriers to these forces of change. Many result from the assumption that Learning by Participation will reduce the power of an institution. LBP does threaten the power of national examination committees and the position of certain teacher-unions, departments of the Ministry of Education, inspectors and subject coordinators in schools would be reduced. Learning by Participation is more difficult for administrators and inspectors to control than traditional education, and the reduction of central guidelines is a difficult obstacle.

Learning By Participation also reduces the power of the school over the student. The student takes more decisions and the teacher must share influence over the learning process with other adults. Sometimes a school sets up conditions for the out-of-school component so that this component in effect becomes only an extension of the school. These conditions do not facilitate real participation, but prevent it.

The goals of Learning by Participation are not concrete enough for many people. Different interpretations are possible. The reaction of one administrator to an I.C.P. report which gave a more concrete form to the Learning by Participation definition was: 'We know that Learning by Participation is better than the I.C.P.'.

Some schools use the Learning by Participation labels only to pull in extra money. Interest groups contend with each other over the interpretation of the Learning by Participation definition.

Implementation of Learning by Participation affects all aspects of education. One can wonder whether the concept is not too complex for successful school implementation: there is a great lack of expertise; teachers often know very little about the local community and the world of work; they are not sure they know how to make contact with persons and organizations outside the educational system; specialists in curriculum development have no experience of Learning by Participation programmes; there are no adequate evaluation techniques. What is an effective approach to reduce conflicts of interest? How can one prevent a bureaucratization of the innovation process? How should one react to the impact of increasing youth unemployment on the process? How should one respond to the fear of exploitation of students as cheap labourers? And so forth. Every central innovation meets a host of implementation problems. One cannot expect that the goals of the three plans of the I.C.P. can be reached only through a central approach. The main functions of the national innovation project Learning by Participation in the Netherlands are probably to ensure that the following developments are maintained and furthered:

there is now a great deal of discussion concerning Learning by Participation both within and outside the school system;
many people are now aware of an alternative to the present situation;
there is now a climate for all kinds of Learning by Participation initiatives at the school level;
teachers and specialists can use a conceptual framework for the development of programmes;
local initiatives have been affirmed and have a greater chance to survive;

more (though not enough) resources are available;
education at the upper secondary level is in movement. There are
guidelines for change processes and in many situations much
energy and creativity is invested in the improvement of
educational practice.

For many people within the educational system it is no longer
necessary to be defensive against attacks on the system. One can now
react positively to the criticism by changing the way schools help
people to develop.

This description of the national project Learning by Participation
in the Netherlands is not a systematic analysis. It is more a subjective
and impressionistic picture by an insider. The processes are very
complicated, with thousands of factors influencing the outcome.
Existing descriptions concern only a part of the process or are
written on a very abstract level. A systematic description, analysis
and evaluation of the work of the I.C.P. and the situations in which
this group operates would be very relevant. This can only be done
by a sophisticated outsider. It would give more insight into both the
Learning by Participation movement and the dynamics of
educational change.

Local initiatives

Six teachers, who work at different academically-oriented schools in
Amsterdam and Amersfoort, developed a programme which started
in 1977 called 'work-experience learning' in which students worked
for one or two weeks in a factory or shop. This period was prepared
and also evaluated intensively over several months. For the space of
one year, all the activities in the course of the teacher concerned were
linked with this project. Questionnaires were developed as well as
interview schedules and concepts for the analysis of experiences.
The students, it is hoped, gain some insight into the world of work
and learn to analyse their own experiences. One problem with this
programme is that the students' activities are not directly useful for
society, and a second is that the programme takes up only a small
part of the students' school time, and bears no relation to the
teaching of other courses.

Some small but successful projects are known as 'project

decision'. Within the limits of one or two courses a student participates in a project that is socially useful. Examples include research and action with regard to the pollution of the natural environment, and the establishment of a service for handicapped children. One group of students and their teacher are aiming to accomplish better housing conditions for foreign workers. Although these programmes give an alternative for education in only one or two subject disciplines in one year, they do offer ways of implementing Learning by Participation at school level.

In academically-oriented schools, especially, students might spend some weeks of the year on an independent study project, usually in small groups. These projects can be used as a means of explaining the goals of Learning by Participation.

In every educational system one can find idealistic and creative teachers, who apply Learning by Participation without any conceptual framework. One teacher based a course of two years on archaeological excavation, and the publication and exhibition of the results.

In another school some students and their teacher constructed a windmill which delivers electricity; in a vocational programme in electronics, students designed and constructed speech amplifiers for eight people who had lost their vocal chords through an operation. In the same school, a group of students is constructing an alarm system in a home for old people.

Local Learning by Participation initiatives without any central support are exceptions in the centralized Dutch system. However, these exceptions contain a promise for the future, if centralization can be reduced. The strength of local initiatives is the direct relationship that they have with practice. There are few, if any, barriers between the innovator and the practitioner. Very often they are the same person. The weakness of these initiatives lies in continuity. Very often a programme disappears, for example, because a teacher moves. Implementation is also limited to one or a few schools, whereas the life and dissemination of local initiatives can be promoted by relationships with national projects. As we described above, this is a conscious strategy in the national Learning by Participation project. This relationship has sometimes very positive effects on local people (we are recognized) as well as on the national innovators (who get concrete feedback on their concepts).

Sometimes it gives rise to problems. A teacher can feel a

programme is his emotional property and it can be difficult for him to accept that other schools can have access to his programme, without many of the problems he has had to solve. A second problem is that the national innovators try to convince teachers to improve the programme, and by doing this, teachers can loosen their emotional relationship with it. The latter problem can be prevented, if the national innovators approach a local initiative more as learners than as critics or experts.

Prospects for Learning by Participation in the Netherlands

The topic Learning by Participation plays an important role in discussions of the educational system. This chapter is limited to Learning by Participation in upper secondary education. One sees also some movement and interest for Learning by Participation in other parts of the system. However, only at the upper secondary level can one speak of a coordinated and braod movement.

Although a national project has many disadvantages and causes many implementation problems, this project is of great importance for the implementation and dissemination of Learning By Participation in the Netherlands. Earlier in this chapter I stressed that the key issue was the relationship between the two levels of central control and the school. How, then, can the two movements reinforce each other?

Central persons have to be willing to learn by participation in local activities. Local persons have to be willing to learn by participation in national activities. These linkage functions must *not* be filled by special persons or agencies, but by an overlap of the two kinds of activities and by the networks of the people most closely involved. For example, local persons have to be involved in the work of the National Committee for Learning by Participation and central innovators have to cooperate with schools in the planning of school programmes.

The Learning by Participation movement began during a period of very favourable economic conditions. This climate has changed. The central trade unions have changed their priorities, and for them the most important goal is now the protection of the jobs of their members. They now have an ambivalent attitude towards Learning by Participation. Politicians want to use Learning by Participation as a means to keep young people longer in the educational system; employers see in Learning by Participation a chance to realize some of their wishes. The support of the people who work in the educational system is increased. Programmes at school level stimulate the support of students and parents. However, Learning by Participation should not become too dependent on people within the school system. People from outside the schools must be involved in the implementation process.

More and more, young people stay in the educational system for longer. Partly because of this, the relationship between the length of someone's school career and his socio-economic position has become weaker. One already hears of 'over-schooling', meaning that people learn more than they need for the jobs they can obtain. We do not think this is a real problem. The structure of the labour market has already, for too long, determined the educational system. Learning by Participation gives schools insight into educational functions, which do not have a direct relationship with future occupations.

In traditional education the emphasis is on learning processes which seek to adjust the learner to future social situations. Learning by Participation emphasizes the contribution of students to the adjustment of present social situations to the values of people. It helps to make people a little less powerless by fostering social structures that people create for themselves.

Reports coming from the experimental schools, and my own observations, suggest that the enthusiasm of parents and other adults who are involved with Learning By Participation programmes is becoming stronger. The enthusiastic reactions of businesses and individuals having had experience of LBP programmes stand in contrast to the statement made by one representative of a national organization to the effect that the world of work is not suited to an educational mission. Students demonstrate not only that they can be very useful in society but that more humane ways than the professionals want us to believe are possible.

In the short term the Learning by Participation movement has to find a solution to its problems with the examination structures. In most schools, students finish their careers with an examination. These examinations are organized by national examination committees, which make up the questions. In one moment a student is judged on his or her learning process over years and in many subject disciplines. This, of course, has a great impact on school practice. Many teachers fear that Learning by Participation will reduce a student's chances of passing an exam.

It seems from the Learning by Participation concept that it is desirable to replace the whole central examination system by a credit system at the school level which will be centrally coordinated only. However, this is a very radical change. It is necessary to work on this change, but it is only possible gradually, through a step-by-step strategy. It will take a lot of time. After difficult negotiations a decentralized credit system has been accepted for the above-mentioned new vocational programmes.

Most Learning by Participation programmes must find provisional solutions at the school level. Some solve the problem in such a way that every student is obliged to attend a number of traditional courses. Another solution is that a school formulates exactly which sorts of knowledge, insights and skills a student needs to pass the traditional examination. The learning programme of every student is checked, to see whether these learning goals are included and when this is not possible in a Learning by Participation programme the student must follow a traditional course. In a third solution, a school gets permission from the central level for an examination procedure deviating from the norm. The latter solution can have a negative impact on the image of the school. An advantage of the first two solutions is that it can be demonstrated that Learning by Participation programmes at least meet the same learning goals as traditional education. A ray of hope may be found in the increasing criticism of the investment of money, time and manpower in the yearly organization of national examinations.

The future of Learning by Participation in the Netherlands is difficult to predict. One can emphasize the barriers or one can emphasize the forces for change. What is certain is that Learning by Participation has a role to play in the Dutch system, though it is still uncertain how it will be implemented and on what scale. Learning by Participation is not an autonomous movement. It is connected with other movements, which are also looking for answers to the over-institutionalization, alienation, specialization and disintegration of our society. The future of Learning by Participation is in a large measure connected with the future of this broader social reform.

Notes and References

1. For an extended description of the school see: 'Experimenteerverslag 1975-1979', De Groene School, Amsterdam Plantage Doklaan 14 (unpublished).
2. For an extended description of the programme see: 'Leren participerend leren.' Tuindorpschool, 636 Postbus, Hengelo (unpublished).
3. NUYTEN-EDELBROEK, E.G.M. (1977): *Het is slecht gesteld met de middelbare scholier*, Rotterdam: Erasmus University. See also LIPPENS, B.C. (1976): *Klackten van leerlingen op schoolgemeenschappen* v.w.o.-h.a.v.o. Eindhoven.
4. The goals of these reforms are described in a government memorandum *Contouren van een toekomstig onderwijsbestel.* juni 1975, Staatsuitgeverij, 's-Gravenhage.
5. See also: *Eerste advises van de Innovatiecommissie Participatie-onderwijs: Hoofdlijnen van een innovatieplan.* augustus 1976, Staatsuitgeverij, 's-Gravenhage.
6. A detailed description of this definition is given in a report of the Innovatiecommissie Participatie-onderwijs: *Participerend leren: een andere leerweg, deel I.* oktober 1978, Staatsuitgeverij, 's-Gravenhage.
7. The design of this strategy is described in a report of the I.C.P.: *Tweede advises van de Innovatiecommissie Participatie-onderwijs: De stimuleringsstrategie*, 1977, Straatsuitgeverij, 's-Gravenhage.
8. Innovatiecommissie Participatie-onderwijs: *Participerend leren: een andere leerweg*, 3 bundels, 7 delen, oktober 1978, Straatsuitgeverij, 's-Gravenhage.
9. See, for example, the reports: *Participerend leren in Noord-Amerika en Engeland*, I.C.P., januari 1978. *Verslag van een oriëntatiebezoek aan de Sanct Annagadeschool te Arhus*, I.C.P., mei 1979.
10. The I.C.P. published two reports about the design of this strategy, namely: *Het derde advies* and *Zesde advies*. See list for further reading.

List of further reading

All the publications are in the Dutch language.

1. INNOVATIECOMMISSIE PARTICIPATIE-ONDERWIJS: *Participerend leren: een andere leerweg,*
    Deel I: Analyse en vergelijking vvan zes projekten,
    Deel II, III, IV: Buitenlandse projekten,
    Deel V, VI, VII: Nederlandse projekten.
    oktober 1978, Staatsuitgeverij, 's-Gravenhage. The most important publication in Dutch about Learning by Participation. Deel I contains detailed description of the definition and describes the conditions at school level for the implementation of Learning by Participation. Deel

II through VII contains case descriptions.

2. INNOVATIECOMMISSIE PARTICIPATIE-ONDERWIJS: Eerste advies: *Hoofdlijnen van een innovatieplan.* augustus 1976, Staatsuitgeverij, 's-Gravenhage. This report describes the philosophical basis of the national innovation project Learning by Participation.

3. INNOVATIECOMMISSIE PARTICIPATIE-ONDERWIJS: Derde advies: *De ontwikkelingsstrategie.* augustus 1977, Staatsuitgeverij, 's-Gravenhage. This report desribes proposals for a central policy to support school by the development of Learning by Participation programmes.

4. INNOVATIECOMMISSIE PARTICIPATIE-ONDERWIJS: Zesde advies: *Nadere voorstellen over de ontwikkelingsstrategie.* juni 1979, Zeist. A report about a central strategy to implement Learning by Participation at the school level. The report gives a detailed framework for the implementation of Learning by Participation in vocational programmes.

5. INNOVATIECOMMISSIE PARTICIPATIE-ONDERWIJS: Tweede advies: *De stimuleringsstrategie.* 1977, Straatsuitgeverij, 's-Gravenhage. A report about methods to promote Learning by Participation.

6. MINISTERIE VAN ONDERWIJS EN WETENSCHAPPEN: *Naar het participatie-onderwijs.* mei 1975, Straatsuitgeverij, 's-Gravenhage. A report of the Dutch government about the policy concerning Learning by Participation.

7. MINISTERIE VAN ONDERWIJS EN WETENSCHAPPEN: *Contouren van een toekomstig onderwijsbestel,* juni, 1975, Staatsuitgeverij, 's-Gravenhage. A memorandum from the Minister of Education about the future of the Dutch education system. A summary of the memorandum is available in English with the title: 'Contours of a future education system in the Netherlands', 1977, Staatsuitgeverij, 's-Gravenhage.

8. STICHTING UITVOERINGSGROEP STREEKCENTRA: *Raamplan participatie-onderwijs, deel I, II, III en IV.* juni 1977. You can obtain this publication from S.U.S. St. Laurensdreef 49, Utrecht, Netherlands. A catalogue of implementation efforts at the school level.

9. PROJEKTGROEP STIMULERING PARTICIPATIE-ONDERWIJS: Catalogus studiedag participerend leren. 11 mei 1979, Utrecht, St. Laurensdreef 49. Short descriptions of 17 programmes at the school level.

10. JEUGD EN SAMENLEVING themanummer over: *Projektonderwijs.* oktober 1978, Utrecht. A description of 7 local programmes.

11. VAN DEN BOSCH, L.J. (1975): 'Onderwijs aan werkende jongeren'. *Intermediair,* 11^e jaargang 45, 7 november 1975, Amsterdam. An analysis of the policy of the Dutch government towards Learning by Participation.

12. VAN DEN BOSCH, L.J. (1973): 'Experimenten participatie-onderwijs: welke lading dekt deze vlag?' *Jeugd en Samenleving,* februari 1973,

Utrecht. An analysis of the first efforts of Learning by Participation at the school level.

13. VAN DEN BOSCH, L.J. (1975): 'Evalueren van onderwijsinnovaties', *Pedagogische Studien*, 1975 (52), 128-140. Wolters-Noordhof, Groningen. A description of evaluation approaches of central innovation.

14. GEURTS, J. EN TESSER, P. (1976): *Werkende jongeren en hun onderwijs*, Link Nijmegen. A research report about characteristics of the social situation of early school leavers.

15. KOOPS, I. en RAE, V. (1977): *Experimenteren met participerend leren*, maart Kohnstamm-Instituut, Amsterdam. A description of 5 experimental schools which implement Learning by Participation.

16. JONKERGOUW, TH. (1973): *Participatie-onderwijs in opbouw*, Samson, Alphen aan de Rijn. A description of the organizations which are involved in the first years of the innovation project participatory education.

CHAPTER THREE
The United Kingdom

NOEL KERSHAW

In complete contrast to the centralized system of the Netherlands, a strong tradition of localism in the educational systems of the United Kingdom has permitted substantial levels of latitude for innovative practice at the school level. Another source of innovation is in local non-school agencies serving, primarily, out-of-school young people. The role of these latter agencies has taken on new importance as the UK struggles to contend with severe unemployment and attendant alienation among young people. Although the tendency towards local problem-solving with little central coordination (at least with regard to LBP) has made it difficult to gauge the scope of LBP programmes, a project sponsored by the government Further Education Curriculum Review and Development Unit has been compiling a 'Register of Innovative Practice in Experiential and Participatory Education' in England and Wales. This project, which is also producing a 'Guide to Best Practice' is directed by Noel Kershaw, who contributes the following chapter. Mr Kershaw served as Deputy Principal of Nelson and Colne College, a leader in the UK for instituting experiential learning programmes.

Definition

Participatory learning is a valuable refinement of experiential education, although the two terms are not synonymous in that while all participatory learning is experiential the reverse is by no means true. For instance a typical experiential learning situation in the United Kingdom is provided by the average school/college link-course during which the students experience practical work which they have never undertaken before in, perhaps, engineering or hairdressing or the construction trade. Very often, however, they have no choice in the departments in which they work, as they are on a 'taster' course, spending some time in each section taking part, and there is no sense of the students having any real involvement or responsibility. Much the same can be said of a great deal of work experience which takes place in factories or on commercial premises.

If an experiential learning situation is also to be participatory the students first of all need to be a part of the planning process. This does not mean of course that they should be presented with a situation and simply told to get on with it, but that they are given an opportunity to discuss the form which the experience will take and to feel that their views are being taken into account. This process should not stop once the programme is put into operation but should allow for continuous modification in the light of the students' findings. In educational terms, the purpose of this participation is to relate experience and theoretical learning by guided reflection on the former.

Encouraging participation of this kind almost certainly means that there will be a change in the teacher/student relationship and particularly in the role of the teacher. If the students take some share in decision-making then the teacher's share must necessarily be less. This does not of course mean that his role will be easier – in fact it is likely to become more complex as a result, although to compensate for this, releasing students' abilities can sometimes be more rewarding than directing them.

Participatory learning implies not only student involvement but also participation in society. The immediate goal may not be to pass an examination or obtain a grade, but to add to the welfare of pre-school children, old people or adolescents with problems – or to produce a useful product or give a service to a satisfactory standard and within specific cost and time limits. The underlying goal of such participation however, will usually be to give students greater responsibility:
a)   in making decisions affecting others – including the group with whom they may be working;
b)   in being accountable for their actions;
c)   in being able to experience the consequences of their actions, including failure.
All this is done through the medium of practical activity which students find socially useful, challenging and intrinsically rewarding.

As described here, learning by participation does not exist in an organized way in the United Kingdom although there are trends in that direction. It is necessary to look at the system of education and at current attitudes toward it to see why this should be so.

Although there are some variations the most usual patterns are demonstrated in Table 2 below. Education is compulsory between the ages of five and sixteen and normally the first six years take place in infant and junior schools. At eleven there is a transfer to the secondary stage. In those areas where a form of selection still takes place at this age some 20 to 25 per cent of pupils will go to a Grammar School and the remainder to a Secondary Modern School. Where re-organization has taken place all students transfer to non-selective comprehensive schools.

Table 2

A Brief Outline of the United Kingdom Education System

Age 5		11		16		18
Stage	Primary		Secondary		Tertiary	
Type of Institution	Infant and Junior schools	Selective	– Grammar Schools – Modern Schools		– Grammar Schools	
		Non-Selective	– Comprehensive Schools		– Comprehensive Schools	
					Further Education Colleges	
		Compulsory Education			Sixth Form Colleges	

The majority of students at whatever kind of school sit one of two nationally-accepted examinations – the Ordinary level of the General Certificate of Education (G.C.E. 'O' level), or the Certificate of Secondary Education (C.S.E.). The highest grade of pass in the Certificate of Secondary Education is regarded as equivalent to the lowest level of pass in the G.C.E. 'O' level.

At sixteen students can either stay at a Grammar School or Comprehensive School in what is known as the 6th form, usually to take examinations for the Advanced level of the General Certificate of Education (G.C.E. 'A' level), normally taken after two years study. They may, however, at sixteen transfer to a separate academic 6th form College, again specializing mainly in the G.C.E. 'A' level examination or they have the option of transferring to a College of Further Education in which they can take either G.C.E. 'A' level or a wide variety of craft and vocational courses.

The Educational Context

The Schools. Although individual schools in the United Kingdom, such as A.S. Neill's Summerhill, have a long history of running projects of an experiential and participatory nature, no support at a national level was given to this kind of approach until the publication of the Newsom Report *Half our Future* in 1963.[1] A phrase such as 'learning by participation' might have meant nothing to the authors of the report but they did make a number of statements entirely consistent with its principles. At its most basic the final words of the chapter on *Objectives* were:

> it may be useful to say at once that we foresee the need, especially as older boys and girls stay on at school, to extend considerably the provision for activities outside the formal lesson programme, and to draw a less sharp line between what is learnt in and what is learnt outside the classroom.

This is certainly a licence for schools to pursue experiential projects and further precise encouragement is given to student involvement – 'one way of marking approaching adult status is to give the curriculum a new look for the last two years of school life and to allow pupils themselves some choice . . . . . in the kind of programme they follow'. There is also some indication of the possible nature of that involvement – 'a few Heads suggest that a less authoritarian organization may be more appropriate to present day concepts, and are anxious to find ways in which all the older pupils can be given personal responsibility. One way may lie through community service projects'. Finally Newsom makes it quite clear that the external or real life experience should be properly related to the remainder of a student's course:

> the pupils themselves need to go out and explore . . . always they will need good preliminary briefing. Many schools do already arrange excellent programmes of this kind, but there is room for

more experiment in this field, especially in relating the experience . . . . . more closely to the rest of the work in school. The
pupils themselves ought to be brought in as much as possible to
the initial planning and organisation and making of arrangements.
In the management of themselves and their contact with other
people outside the familiar school situation, and in the subsequent
presentation of their experience, they can learn much, quite apart
from any information they may have acquired.

No apology is made for quoting at length since these statements
embody the spirit of participatory learning. Although nowhere
clearly mapping out the details of the experiences to be undertaken
every encouragement is given to schools to experiment with student
involvement in real projects in the world outside. As the report
plainly states 'the school programme, in the last year especially,
ought to be deliberately out-going. This means taking the pupils
mentally and often physically beyond the school walls' and there is
no doubt that, since the report was published, some schools have in
part at least, followed its advice.

It is unfortunate that the opportunity, thrown up by the raising of
the school-leaving age (R.O.S.L.A.) in 1972[2], to re-examine the
curriculum in the way Newsom suggests has, perhaps, never been
properly taken up. Indeed as far as many innovative people within
the school system are concerned, 'R.O.S.L.A. has turned out to be a
disappointment'. This comment was made by White and Brockington
at the beginning of their book *In and Out of School*, describing the
Bristol R.O.S.L.A. project, and they go on to say that the factor
which has been largely ignored 'is the *form* which education takes'.
When one reads seminal documents related to R.O.S.L.A., such as
the Schools Council[3] Working Paper No. 2 which describes the
programme of research and development to be undertaken, this
failure to grasp the nettle of reform is not surprising for, in the
general sections, there is no hint that the relationship between
experience out of school and that in school has any value. The only
reference appears in paragraphs 64 and 65 under the heading
'Operational Problems in the Humanities' and even there, although
it is accepted as necessary 'that the confines of the class rooms are
manifestly broken down', the reference peters out in talk of
discussion groups and residential courses with the earth-shattering
conclusion that 'more comfortable chairs for discussion groups may

have a part to play'. In the face of such official blandness schools
have had to make their own rules in applying Newsom's theories to
any kind of participatory practice. This means that the roots are
there in some programmes in some schools, but they are not
receiving any proper nourishment from national recognition and
approval. It would seem to be time for a re-statement and
development of the views quoted above from the Newsom report.

Further Education. The schools are not of course the only sector in
which experiential learning has been practised. The Further
Education service has itself provided opportunities for many schools
through linked courses, and has also introduced experiential
education into many of its own courses. In this respect one of the
most valuable developments to have been made in Further Education
since 1945 is in the field of Sandwich Courses – that is professional or
technological courses in which theoretical work in the college is
integrated with, and related to, periods of practical work in
commerce and industry.

The Sandwich Course is not Learning by Participation but its
very existence has given Further Education a tradition of offering
courses which involve both in-college and out-of-college elements
and has meant that within the service there are likely to be fewer
barriers to the introduction of innovatory practices which involve
breaking down the boundaries between education and the world
outside.

A number of courses have also for many years now contained an
element of project work; that is, student-directed assignments on a
real life topic area, which has allowed students to make contact with
the outside world as part of their educational programme. In part-
time courses this has often been the means of linking what was
happening in college with the realities of the student's working life.
Once again the pattern created by this educational process is not too
far removed from the strategy of Learning by Participation –
particularly when, as in some supervisory and management courses,
the student's project may lead to actual changes at his workplace.

All of this means that the ideas behind experiential and
participatory learning are not totally foreign to further education and
has for instance resulted in an examining body such as the City and
Guilds[4] being able to produce in its Foundation Course a curriculum
which need not be interpreted in a specific vocational way and which

lends itself, as can be seen later, to a treatment which can encourage student involvement and a flexible attitude towards where learning may take place. This is not to say that there is always encouragement for Learning by Participation in the colleges but the relevant freedom of contact with commerce and industry makes it quite fruitful soil for anyone wishing to develop this approach. This is certainly beginning to be seen in some of the attempts to answer the problems caused by youth unemployment and a number of the examples to be cited spring from this need.

Adult Education. The third strand in British Education which has some relevance to the possibilities of developing participatory programmes is adult education with its traditions of using adult experience of informal learning and community involvement. Some of the recent development of informal learning has been brought about because of the need to tackle illiteracy and the resulting use of volunteeer tutors to facilitate this work. Such an educational pattern is not directly participatory but it does ensure that the resources of the community are used and progress from the classroom and the formal teacher/student relationship.

If education can involve in this way a great variety of people who are not pedagogically trained, then it seems less unreasonable to construct whole programmes which make use of real-life experience, because in order to do this effectively much reliance will at times need to be placed on ordinary members of a community in the same way that this has had to be done in volunteer schemes.

Adult experience is also increasingly being used as the raw material for courses, especially with re-entry programmes of the Open College[5] type. When designing a new syllabus for this kind of student it is the relationship between subjects as demonstrated in everyday life rather than the division between subjects within the academic curriculum that is the important factor. In many areas there has also been a long-standing development of community involvement, perhaps first clearly exemplified in the Cambridgeshire Village Colleges[6]. What is important for Learning by Participation is that many of these developments are now taking place within colleges of further education rather than in separate units. This means that the attitude to learning of the adult educator has a chance to rub off on teachers in other parts of the institutions who are having to develop new courses for the 16- to 19-year-olds.

It can be seen therefore that although there is no clear movement in the United Kingdom towards widespread use of Learning by Participation there are a number of predisposing factors in secondary, further and adult education which can be used by innovators to create relevant projects or elements within a whole course. There is sufficient flexibility within the British education system to do this, although before looking at the kinds of approaches used it will be instructive to compare the situation with that in other countries.

The Value of Experiential and Participatory Learning

The approach to education represented by Learning by Participation is intended to offer to teachers in colleges and schools a variety of methods for:
a)   giving access to renewed education for those who have lost interest or lost heart and
b)   enabling all students to add to their educational experience by learning something of those facets of life best taught outside the classroom.
In relation to both objectives experiential and participatory learning can increase the relevance and the flexibility of the work of a course.

A Relevant Curriculum

The debates on education in the United Kingdom of the mid-seventies were greatly coloured by the idea of relevance. Unfortunately this was all too often limited to direct preparation for the world of work whereas participatory learning has somewhat broader objectives and implies a breaking down of the barriers between the classroom and the whole of the world in which students live. Work is important but it is not the sum total of life and a worthwhile participatory experience can enlarge students' first-hand knowledge of many other facets of their environment.

Life has never been something which can be understood solely from books. Traditionally, however, the academic curriculum has drawn far more from the library than from the factory or the hospital or the market place and this has been true not only for the intellectually able but also of courses produced for students with less aptitude for academic work. Discovery methods and other new approaches may be used in such cases but too often only as part of a watering down of the original content of subjects rather than in taking the opportunity to adopt wider criteria for the curriculum.

Those who favour participatory learning feel that it is essential to redress the balance in education towards a clearer preparation for the realities of life by learning from shared experiences. This applies to students of all levels of ability from those in need of basic education to those capable of some form of Higher Education. There is a danger of placing our young people in a quarantine period before real life begins, or of putting them in an educational deep freeze to be taken out and put back in society at the age of 16, 18, 21 or even later depending on the course they follow.

Youth unemployment has not created the need for greater relevance; it has simply underlined it. If young people are to become more valuable members of society then their education must help them to relate to society at first hand. It is in doing this vitally important job that Learning by Participation can help students to discover themselves, to discover real life problems and their own potential for helping to solve them.

A Flexible Curriculum

Not only the aims of Learning by Participation are important but also the means used to achieve them. It does not matter whether the problems mentioned above are ones of productivity or of social deprivation since to the student it is their reality which is the important factor. It is particularly important when dealing with young people who have rejected formal schooling as such that their full support is engaged both by giving them a chance to do something actively, instead of simply being expected to absorb information, and also by allowing them to be involved in directing the course of their particular project. These needs are just as vital, however, whatever the student's academic ability may be and it would be wrong to restrict the use of such methods only to those in danger of failing to gain employment. If we do this they will quite rightly reject them as some form of second-class programme to be used only with those who have failed once already. All students can gain benefit from the positive experience of doing something constructive, either for or with others, and there are those who would say that some of our national problems are caused by our treating the education of those academically inclined as something quite separate from the other concerns of their life.

Since the experiences on which learning is based can occur anywhere in industry or in the community this greatly increases the resources which the teacher can put at the disposal of his students. It also offers the likelihood that informal assistance can be obtained from non-teachers who have relevant experience to pass on. To some people both these possibilities may be worrying but provided that teachers can remain as the focal point or catalyst of activity, the extra levels of enthusiasm and involvement which such projects generate can more than compensate for any reduction of their over-all control.

Current Practice in the United Kingdom

From what has already been said it will be clear that there is no simple way of cataloguing participatory learning in the United Kingdom because of its fragmented nature. Projects which go some way toward meeting its objectives can be found in all sectors of the education system from universities to programmes for drop-outs from secondary schools. There is also no accepted way of encouraging or financing relevant programmes. In some places funds have been provided through charitable trusts, in others the stimulus has come from non-profit-making educational organizations. The great majority, however, have been provided by educational institutions who have either persuaded their local Authority of the validity of what they were doing and so given it a legitimate place within the curriculum or have found sources of funds from non-educational public bodies such as the Manpower Services Commission[7], which have meant that as far as the education service was concerned they were self-supporting.

These matters are much less important, however, than the central questions of whether the programmes involve the students rather than dictate to them, whether they expose them to some useful situation outside their school or college and whether proper sense is made of that exposure by related learning processes. These structural factors will assist students to have their understanding of adult life enlarged, to be given a proper sense of purpose and to feel some measure of responsibility for what they are doing – large aims, no doubt, but ones which formal education is currently not fully geared to achieve. It is important to remember, of course, that the educational innovators involved are not consciously following a scheme of Learning by Participation but rather, in their attempts to find ways of giving a meaningful curriculum to young people, they have constructed programmes which fulfil its criteria. It is for this reason that it seemed best to distinguish between them by concentrating on the different approaches adopted to this problem, that is different ways of formalizing the relationship between external experience and learning within the institution, rather than by subject area, by kind of school or college or any other mechanical method.

In the following paragraphs eleven different approaches are described. They are not watertight compartments and some projects have elements which would allow them to be placed under more than one heading, in which case they have been listed according to their most striking characteristic. The two largest groupings are concerned with either social action and involvement or with general preparation for the world of work.

Under social action I would list:

The Project approach;

The Survey approach;

The Community Placement approach;

The Social Education approach;

and under general preparation for the world of work:

The Work Experience or preparation approach;

The Unified Vocational Preparation approach;

The Industrial Unit or Workshop approach;

The Commercial Enterprise approach;

The Twinning approach.

Some programmes are most clearly understood by the dominant factors of their organisation and within this last grouping are:

The Activity Centre approach;

The Residential approach.

Not all eleven approaches are equally effective in reaching learning by participation goals. In particular the various forms of Work Preparation can only be regarded as LBP related programmes and will be shown separately as such.

Approaches to Learning by Participation

1. The Project approach.

By the project approach I mean the completion of a defined, practical task as a clear, attainable goal which helps to make sense of real-life experience for young people. This is an attractive method to use in turning students' eyes to the outside world, since for those adults involved, whether teacher, supervisor or member of the public, it will have quite clear parameters, while for the students the objective to be achieved can normally be perceived as being worthwhile and there is attraction and excitement simply in moving towards it. Projects can be fitted into institutional frameworks without too much difficulty but if they are good ones they will certainly spill over into the private time of both staff and students. The major problems are that once the particular goal is reached another project has to be found – although some people are lucky enough to have discovered large projects with a number of secondary goals – and that if the students are on higher level courses there may be conflict between the demand of the project and the feeling of academic staff that the time given to formal learning should not be unduly eroded.

The major sources of interest covered by known projects are related to the environment, care of the young, the sick and the old, construction and communications and within all of them there are great differences to be found in scale, extent and real life involvement and relative importance to the students' total experience.

SOUTH SHIELDS MARINE AND TECHNICAL COLLEGE – THE GARTH PROJECT

A good example of this approach is the College Garth project at South Shields which is offered to former pupils of E.S.N.(M.)[8] schools in the area. The practical objective is to make a park out of the large derelict garden of an old Victorian house which can be used by the public and which allows access to the physically handicapped in particular. The work is broken down into a number of different sections which can provide a target for the various groups who stay for one year at a time. These individual areas include a small open-air theatre, greenhouses, a Japanese garden and a raised garden specially for the benefit of those in wheelchairs. The students are building various features in the park and cultivating the land on the one-and-a-half acre site, which is run very much on real life lines with work programmes, time keeping and deadlines. Flowers, fruit and vegetables are also grown to exhibition standard and then sold at auction. In this part of the world the latter activity has an important social benefit since many of the students will later join a club or institute where the skills of good gardening are held in very high esteem.

During the week students attend the College for a total of six hours split into four sessions. Part of this time is spent on physical education to improve the co-ordination of motor skills, which, in turn, will help their work on the site, and part is concerned with improving their general knowledge of life-skills such as diet, health care, grooming etc. The major portion of the time, however, is related directly to their work on the Garth. Communications and basic maths all spring from problems encountered on site and a major activity is the writing-up of a log book of the tasks they have performed during the week.

Initially the students have to be very much directed but as they gain skills and confidence an increasing amount of responsibility is passed to them. This is in line with the basic aim of the project which is to give the youngsters a skill and the self respect to live in the community with reasonable independence. The success of this enterprise is shown in one way by the fact that the students at the end of the year are able to compete successfully for work with 'normal' school-leavers. Very definite changes have been observed by George Bedell, the project organizer, in the confidence, general manner, ability and maturity of the young people during the five years of the programme's existence. Although there is no formal published work on the Garth as yet, Mr. Bedell is a regular lecturer at University and Regional conferences and is happy to be contacted at the College. The Garth has a long life as there is work in the garden for several years and there are additional developments through the provision of concrete products such as paving flags, decorative walling, etc., for other work experience schemes in the area.

2.   *The Survey approach*
This is, in reality, a special kind of project in that it is a group

activity with a particular goal. Where other projects provide a definite service or have a concrete objective, a survey is a more cerebral activity resulting in a report which may or may not lead to action. Of all the approaches covered this is the most academic and because of that it is useful to consider it separately as a useful method of introducing experiential and participatory learning into the curriculum of more advanced courses.

Because of its greater academic content it can be easier to introduce than many forms of experiential and participatory learning. Although there are examples of the survey approach to be seen within social education programmes and in the work of what I have called activity centres, both dealt with below, surveys as entities in themselves tend to be found in programmes for students of G.C.E. 'O' and 'A' level and above. This may mean that integration with the remainder of the course is rather weak but provided that time is taken to make sense of the practical experience gained during the survey then the value obtained from student involvement and the opportunity for letting some outside fresh air into the course more than outweighs this difficulty.

NORTH HERTFORDSHIRE COLLEGE, HERTFORDSHIRE
CONSERVATION PROJECT (SCIENTIFIC GROUP)
The scientific part of the Hertfordshire Conservation Project was originally devised to employ unemployed natural scientists, graduates in ecology and young people who could not get university or polytechnic places and the intention was to carry out research in connection with various aspects of nature conservation in the county. The main activity was the Hertfordshire Woodlands Survey on which a team of ten was occupied initially for a period of four months. This was a field survey of ancient woodlands in order to determine which woods have the most conservation value and to provide information to organizations such as the Nature Conservancy Council to assist them in acquiring nature reserves or in designating important sites for preservation. Some 420 semi-natural woods in Hertfordshire were surveyed. A habitat map was drawn for each wood, and information on surrounding land use, geology and animals noted and all tree and shrub species recorded.

The Woodland Survey was a continuation of a project originally devised by the Nature Conservancy Council which made the results of a desk survey available. This listed all the woods to be surveyed as identified from early maps, aerial photos and county records. For a three-month period the whole group carried out field work with each team of two people visiting an average of two woods per day, filling in three record sheets for each wood. This involved walking round and through each wood so that all habitats were covered.

After this point the group was divided into three smaller teams, one of which worked on the analysis and reporting of the information discovered by the woodland surveys. The second group carried out field work at a site of special scientific interest where there was a proposal for gravel extraction to take place. Data was compiled about the flora and fauna, for use by the authorities in relation to a public enquiry into the future use of the site. The third team carried out studies of some existing nature reserves about which there was little recorded information.

The work involved produced useful information, some of which led to precise action in the designation of sites for preservation. The students have been able to continue with their scientific studies and indeed some of them have used completed work as a base for research work for further degrees. All of them have been enabled to learn necessary life- and non-employment-skills at first hand through learning to work in a group and to produce practical results within a set time.

The participants were registered college students and were able to be involved in group decisions about the day to day running of the project. Co-operation with various outside bodies such as the education planning departments of Hertfordshire County Council, the Conservation Corps, museums and the Hertfordshire and Middlesex Trust for Nature Conservation has been a major feature of the work. This project has been able to give a large-scale example of an approach which can be used by schools and colleges in a smaller way as an extension of many areas of their work. It is now completed, having operated for approximately twelve months during 1978—9, but information can be obtained from Nigel Agar at North Hertfordshire College.

3.   *The Community Placement approach*
     Community placements are the United Kingdom equivalent of internship in the United States and the title is really self-

explanatory. Young people usually volunteer to be involved in these opportunities to assist in social work of various kinds. Sometimes this work is developed by an individual school and often grows out of a subject area which may have a title such as 'Personal Development Course' or 'Home and Community Studies' but there are a number of areas where there is co-ordination of a wider programme by a youth volunteer organization such as Youth Action Cambridge, or the Volunteer Service Unit at Sevenoaks. It is also one of the areas of work developed by a national agency, Project Trident.

The variety of placements is quite wide – one programme, for instance, lists assistance in psychiatric, geriatric and mental subnormality hospitals, visiting housebound people, helping young backward readers, manual work for old and disabled people and the compilation of a Guide to the area for the physically handicapped. Observable changes in attitude of the young participants are often recorded such as increased respons-ibility, initiative and greater understanding of other people's problems. In qualitative terms, however, perhaps the most important measure is of the amount of preparation for the experience and of opportunities for feed-back during the placement which are open to students and this certainly differs markedly from one school or scheme to another.

Well thought-out schemes involve quite stringent preparation when questions are asked, and answered, about the kind of experience to be undertaken, the learning involved and the action necessary. There is also feed-back and discussion with social workers and members of the community, regular meetings with the area officers, informal gatherings of clients, students and staff and discussion with other community workers. Unfortunately such thoroughness is not always evident but it does at least demonstrate that what is possibly the most valuable pattern is understood and attainable in the United Kingdom.

MERSEYSIDE COMMUNITY SERVICE OPPORTUNITIES

This programme is one response to the enormous problem of unemployment in the Liverpool area. Past experience had suggested that Community Service helped many young people to become more positive about themselves and those around them, and at the time that the Youth Opportunity's programme was originally under discussion Merseyside Community Service Opportunities was set up as a pilot project for Community Service work experience. Three areas were chosen in which to set up bases for the work, namely Halewood, Speke, and Toxteth. All of them had housing and unemployment difficulties although their social mix was somewhat different. The major work of the programme has been in placements.

Any organization involved in servicing the community in some way – hospitals, schools, nurseries, community organisations, homes for the elderly etc. was approached as a potential placement provider in which a young person could work. Not only availability of places had to be investigated but also the willingness of the organization to provide the young people with adequate support, training and supervision. Satisfying this second criterion made the provision of placements more difficult but it was vitally important that the trainees should not be used as free labour.

The scheme is run by a project manager and six development officers, two in each area covered, and it is the development officers who find and assess placements and maintain liaison with staff sited there. The development of this liaison is essential if the trainees are to receive proper support and counselling during their time in the scheme. The normal duration of a traineeship is for a year and if possible two six-month opportunities are given to each trainee.

Merseyside Community Service Opportunities is essentially a scheme of training and development which attempts to provide a stimulus through which young people can discover and develop their interests and capabilities. The educational process involved takes a number of forms. On-the-job training is an integral part of the programme and experience of working conditions is useful, of itself, for unemployed young people: for example, the fact that someone depends on your turning up for work, having a routine, the necessity of having a good relationship with colleagues. The importance of more formal education is also stressed and trainees are encouraged to attend relevant college courses. In addition to all this a great deal of informal counselling is provided by the development officers and also by those who supervise trainees at their work.

4. *The Social Education approach*

This is very much a total approach and can involve elements to be found in each of the three previous sections which become part of an action-oriented, year-long school programme. Good examples of such schemes have been identified in Birmingham, Sheffield and Watford and in each a part of the school curriculum, typically 10 to 15 per cent, is re-structured in a very flexible fashion so that group decisions as to its direction can be followed up.

The direction of the course is usually in the hands of an education worker from a non-statutory youth organization who works with a member of the school staff. The over-all aim is to take a social studies syllabus and to illustrate it by use of practical involvement in the community – and in order to do this the teachers and others involved have to accept that they will be used as a resource rather than being in full control and between the periods of greatest involvement for the students there must be more than adequate time for discussion of the issues raised.

Student participation can vary from standard community service placements in playgroups, hospitals and old people's homes to running a food co-operative for pensioners, initiating enquiries into community problems and video and photographic projects. The elements which differentiate this approach are first, that the surveys, placements or projects are not seen at all as ends in themselves but as part of a larger over-all pattern of experience which attempts to make greater sense of the community as a whole and of the individual's place in it, and second, the joint staffing of the whole programme with the school placing responsibility on a non-staff member. There is also a deliberate attempt to develop life skills such as conservation, communication, analysis and diagnosis and other social skills such as co-operation, organization, self-confidence and sensitivity to others. These matters are not really susceptible to examination although some continuous assessment is possible.

As can be seen social education programmes encourage student participation in deciding the direction of the project. Typically the strategy is to begin with a careful look at the surrounding community and then to encourage small groups to follow up particular interests. Suggestions by staff are taken up and developed by students – in a project looking at Race Relations in an area of Birmingham, the students themselves decided who to interview and what were the right questions to ask. There is no doubt that social education schemes have aims and structures which relate exactly to the criteria of experiential and participatory learning and it is interesting to note that this approach has also been tried with success by sixth-form academic students in their minority time rather than being seen as something only suitable for the academically less-gifted.

BIRMINGHAM YOUNG VOLUNTEERS SOCIAL EDUCATION PROJECT

Social education is an integrated process which attempts to increase self, group and community understanding for young people. In the Birmingham project, as in most others, all the sessions are located outside normal school premises and they are conducted on a team basis by a teacher and an education worker from Birmingham Young Volunteers. The sessions normally last for at least two hours, sometimes for a full half day and take place in community centres or some kind of hired room. Simulations and role play, easy access to the locality and use of its resources for surveys, for information and for projects all form part of the programme activities. The structure of the sessions encourages students to be as self-directed as possible.

The pupils involved in this work come from a number of Birmingham Comprehensive schools, each school working as an independent entity. The groups have varied from 4th and 5th year middle-stream pupils to sixth-formers taking part during their Elective Studies periods. The latter groups obviously had a much higher level of educational achievement than the former and so the approach had to be tailored to suit the particular clientele from each school. Annual reports published by Birmingham Young Volunteers[9] clearly demonstrate that it is possible to operate this kind of programme at very different levels.

The B.Y.V. worker and the teacher plan as a team for each school group, weekly. The ideal aim is for total pupil-involvement but in reality pupils' often low expectations of themselves have to be tackled first. Pupil decision-making, planning and organization take place through activities suggested to them and often they then decide subsequent directions they wish to take.

This involves a lot of small group work; for instance, in one of the schools during 1977-8 a number of activities were carried out related to old people in the area. This work resulted from specific pupil requests at the end of the preceding year which determined the direction of their course. Following visits from outside speakers and group discussion, students who volunteer work either at a centre for the elderly or in the geriatric wards of a local hospital. The use of the hospital once again was a follow-up to ideas raised in student discussion. Another group from the same class looked at the problems faced by people living in high-rise flats. This also emerged from work in small group discussions and eventually it led to a wheelchair survey which involved a whole class.

In this survey wheelchairs were borrowed from the social services and teams visited different areas of the city to find out whether access was or was not possible. The teams reported back on their findings and wrote up their results. These were later sent to local newspapers and were made use of in articles which highlight the problems of the disabled. This survey demonstrates quite well the methods used in the social education project which begins with group questioning, moves on to finding out facts related to the problem, returns to further reflection and discussion and eventually, where possible, turns ideas into action.

5.   *The Activity Centre approach*

One very good way in which Learning by Participation can be promoted is through an Activity Centre – that is a non-formal location in which there is clear student involvement in the organization and which encourages a variety of mainly informal approaches to education. Centres of this kind are beginning to appear in both the school and further education sectors.

Possibly the most valuable lead for the future from this kind of enterprise is the way in which some centres act as dual projects – involving students from Higher Education working as volunteers and getting credit for part of their course and also school students who are the target group at whom both staff and volunteers are aiming. For instance, at Hoyland Hall, more fully described below, there is a regular programme of community education projects in which the volunteer students and fifth-form pupils working as a team research into local problems such as subsidence, living on new housing estates, re-housing and slum clearance and despoilation of neighbouring beauty spots. There is also a project in which pupils work alongside college students who are teaching primary school students on informal projects – a situation in which there has to be co-operation throughout the 8 to 22 age-range.

Hoyland Hall is perhaps an extreme example in its variety of provision and in the way in which it has woven itself into the fabric of its community but it represents an approach to the problem of genuine life-skill education for young people which is becoming increasingly of interest in the United Kingdom. The Old Fire Station in Coventry on the other hand works on the principle of the open door, with the attraction of the social centre acting as an enticement to the young people to lead them into the various work preparation courses on offer. The staff at O.F.S. make continuous efforts to involve youngsters in the running of the centre but with only spasmodic success because of the often transient nature of their involvement with their clients and also because of a shortage of staff time. The Bristol R.O.S.L.A. project has been more fortunate in that their contacts with youngsters extend at least for a year and they have also been able to make use of student volunteers in the same way as Hoyland Hall to give a very favourable staff/student relationship. As can be seen development work is still needed but there is tremendous potential for participatory learning within these centres.

HOYLAND HALL PROJECT

Hoyland Hall is in the mining village of Hoyland in South Yorkshire surrounded by a large housing estate. It is a three-storied house which will accommodate 24 people and contains workrooms, student kitchen and dining room, common rooms, warden's flat, bedrooms and a large cellar which has been converted into a youth club with its own entrance. It is used principally by students from the College of Ripon and York St. John but also by children from local schools, teachers, groups from the local community and groups from other parts of the country. They live and work together at the house for periods ranging from a weekend to a month or for two days a week for a whole term. It attempts to be a community education centre for the provision of education through the community.

In particular the Hall is attempting to develop as a centre for adolescents with which they will identify. This involves unattached youth work and an advice centre. There is also a deliberate attempt to develop community work in the area since the Hall is used by local people as well as by students. Also many of the courses involve projects which encourage involvement in the life of the area. This also means that alternative approaches to learning are initiated. In particular contact can be made between students and children as individuals and in small groups, which can be much more revealing than conventional classroom procedures.

The activities which promote these different approaches include the youth club, meetings of local groups and organizations, weekends for handicapped children run by the youth club and use of the premises as a club for a local motor cycle club. In addition there are weekends for local brass bands, meetings of the one-parent family action group, use by intermediate treatment groups from neighbouring cities, and residential weekends both for local schools and for organizations such as the Truancy Centre in the East End of London. This is only a part of the list but it clearly illustrates the multi-faceted approach of the Hall. It also shows the way in which such an activity centre can make one course or project serve another. The community acts as a resource for the students who in turn can bring help to the community. The school children learn from the students who in turn learn from the children.

6. *The Residential approach*

A final method of giving a form to experiential and participatory learning is by making use of residence. Normally this is for a fairly short period which may be either time out from a course or a total experience which has been designed to stand on its own. An interesting example of the first kind is the Hampton House residential course in Belfast in which groups from mixed Catholic and Protestant backgrounds are involved in community placements and shared communal living for a week as a way of illuminating their social work at school. On the other hand, the Corby Outdoor group, although developed from the Further Education College, has no specific relationship with any course or class and exists as a means of developing the experiences of deprived youngsters in the town. The simple act of taking them to a new locality is almost exciting enough for many of those involved but the leaders are attempting to teach enjoyment of the environment and hence a positive respect for it.

A fruitful development of this approach can be seen at Dartington Hall in Devon where a Youth Opportunity work experience programme has been centred around residence in a hostel attached to the College. The Dartington residential programme is for 26 weeks and will obviously not be immediately transferrable to other locations because of the cost involved and the need to obtain a suitable sponsor. There is however plenty of scope for taking advantage in miniature of the benefits offered by this kind of approach and short residential experiences are being planned as part of the educational content of a number of work experience programmes. More extended residence for Higher Education students is one factor in the makeup of a centre such as Hoyland Hall, mentioned in the previous section, where the experience of both working and living in an environment new to the student, together with the development of group spirit, is an important part of the course. The particular value to be gained from residence – that it can help to give such concentrated doses of participatory learning – is another development which needs greater promotion in the United Kingdom, and it is again encouraging to see emphasis placed on it in *A Better Start in Working Life*.[10]

DARTINGTON HALL WORK EXPERIENCE PROGRAMME

This programme has created a situation in which the trainees are responsible for the running of the hostel in which they live and for certain projects during the course of their time there. It also offers plenty of opportunity for informal feedback and group discussion.

About 30 youngsters aged 16 to 18 on MSC (Manpower Services Commission) sponsored courses recruited through the County Careers Service from the whole of Devon are accommodated and the hostel becomes the social centre for the programme, being self-administered as far as possible. This includes operation of the food store, purchase of food, preparation, pricing and selling of breakfasts and packed lunches, general housekeeping, social disciplines and social and recreational events. Most youngsters are resident from Monday until Friday but there is also frequent use of the accommodation at the weekend. The programme usually involves three placements, the first two being quite brief, of one to two weeks only, intended to get youngsters used to normal work routines and for them to examine their reactions to work. There is also a one-week induction course taken by half the group at a time, which allows them to look critically at their own particular problems, to meet employers from various businesses and to carry out an initial project to give them a first appreciation of their capabilities. After this, the major placement is chosen and they are likely to be in that work with increasing amounts of job training until the end of the programme. Placements are offered in a wide variety of locations, many of them associated with Dartington, such as the Dartington farm, Woodlands, retail and estates shops, lithographic printers, Amenity Research Trust, play group, saw mills, tweed manufacturers and Cranks Health Food Restaurant. There are also a number of other placements with local firms, principally in the construction and building industries.

The induction course has the following objectives: to examine critically the reasons why young people are unemployed and specifically what they can do about it; to meet a number of employers from various businesses to discuss types of work opportunities and to hear at first hand what employers are looking for; to carry out project work which gives them a first appreciation of their capabilities and to enable the Programme Director to spend a complete week getting to know all participants.

Throughout the 26 weeks a number of special events and projects are organized. These include the organization of two buffet/social events for invited guests which are entirely the responsibility of the trainees. Close attention is paid to techniques necessary for job finding including counselling sessions both by programme staff and the careers service, training in interview technique and short courses designed to provide each with their own job-application package. The youngsters are encouraged to involve themselves in some of the tremendous variety of cultural and recreational activities centred on Dartington and several of them have had their own weekly drama workshop. They also take part in one-day educational visits to the Midlands and London and in the penultimate week attend a three-day programme run at Brathay Hall in Cumbria. Here they are split into groups quite different from those which they formed at Dartington and considerable demands are made upon their individual initiative. Not only do they have to choose a project and use unfamiliar skills to complete it, they also have to meet an interview panel at which they must argue the case for the value of their chosen project. As can be seen, this is far more than a work preparation programme and its major effects on students are brought about by the developmental nature of the residential situation both at Dartington and encapsulated at Brathay.

The following are best described as Learning by Participation related approaches.

7.   *Work Experience or Work Preparation approach*
Because of the current economic and social situation, programmes which are based on the idea of work preparation or experience are widespread in the United Kingdom. It is immediately necessary to say that only those projects whose aims are general, in the sense of concentrating on personal development rather than on specific vocational training, can normally be considered within a survey of experiential and participatory learning.

The majority of this work tends to be with youngsters who are disadvantaged in some way or who have been educational under-achievers. This means in the first place that it is essential to make attempts to create a situation which has obvious differences from the school life which they have either rejected or found in some way too demanding and therefore the element of placement in a workshop or office is more of a carrot to induce student interest than it is training for that particular job. There is no doubt that many work-experience programmes in the United Kingdom have general life-skill training as a major component.

Typical course patterns include one day per week in work-placements or a short block of two to four weeks placement or the reverse situation in which, after an induction period, students are four days a week at work and on one day have related studies which to some degree attempt to build on the students' out-of-college experience. An initial problem has been to get a clear relationship between the two parts of the course and the amount of success in achieving this aim is a vital factor in ensuring that students get the greatest possible benefit. Apart from various forms of discussion technique many projects make use of some kind of log book as a basis from which to work. Thus the students' own impressions and ideas must of necessity be incorporated into their course. It would be only fair to say however, that opportunities for full participation in the work experience element, in the sense of being able to influence its direction, are not always open to the young people involved. This is such an important and growing part of the educational scene in the United Kingdom that it is vital to find examples of good practice which allow Learning by Participation to play a part in young people's experience.

BARNFIELD COLLEGE, LUTON, PREPARATION FOR WORK

Among the work preparation courses currently being operated many take the opportunity to develop young people in a much wider sense than their rather limiting title might imply. A well organized course such as that at Barnfield College includes among its general aims items such as:

to improve, extend and diversify the capacity to communicate and receive communication;

to improve powers of appraisal and discrimination and the capacity to apply knowledge and skill already possessed to the solution of practical and personal problems;

to encourage greater sensitivity and responsibility in personal relationships with other people;

to help them to discover and develop their powers of creativity and initiative whether at work or at leisure, to provide a broad educational base, including numeracy and literacy.

No doubt this is idealistic but certainly the ideals involved would seem to be valuable ones which are fulfilling the wider purpose for which the Youth Opportunities programme was originally set up.

The guiding principles of this work preparation course are that the content should be student-based as opposed to subject-based, that the course should be relevant to the student's employment situation and that they should have a simple and realistic basis but beyond that be of extreme flexibility to meet individual needs. In practice this means the course involves a 20 per cent element of work-experience placement in local industry, commerce and service. The job training and practical elements in the remainder of the course also aim towards products and services of a marketable standard. In some instances orders are taken and otherwise a range of products is chosen for sale on the free market. The work experience is an integral part of the course and as a matter of routine it is both anticipated through preparatory sessions and reflected upon afterwards. All literacy and numeracy work is functional and as far as possible uses material from the practical situations encountered in the remainder of the programme.

Students have a definite involvement in their course. They choose many of the products mentioned above. They have a course committee with a chairman and other officers, at which tutors are simply in attendance. To date all their major resolutions regarding the course have been able to be acted upon. As can be seen what is involved here is not so much a course of limited skill preparation but rather a programme of general preparation for decision-making in life. Work-preparation courses which do not aim as highly as this would seem to be failing their students in quite a significant manner.

8.   *The Unified Vocational Preparation approach*

This is a kind of reverse experiential approach in that the participants are not going beyond formal education for experience but are taking experience from their job back into their course. There is an attempt to use this experience of young people at work who would not normally be involved in training programmes as the basis for a course which, as in the previous section, aims at both general development and improvement in particular skills. It is worth noting separately as it is the only national initiative in this field directly supported by the Department of Education and Science and as such can help to ensure wider acceptance of the general principles of experiential and participatory learning. Indeed, in the consultative document *A Better Start in Working Life*[10] which looks at the development of U.V.P., participatory teaching/learning methods are given an important place in the brief section on course activities.

As this course content must largely grow out of matters related to the students' working lives and as they often need the freedom to ask questions at their workplace about matters other than those which immediately concern them, it is obvious that this approach can only succeed if there is proper liaison and good understanding between the college lecturers and the industrial supervisors involved. If this partnership works correctly then it can have very valuable results. As one department store manager said of a student, – 'He has developed so much on the course that it would be wrong to keep him in his original limited job and we have rearranged the work of his department to give him more responsibility and more opportunity to display some initiative'. Once again it is the improvement in life skills rather than technical skills that is emphasized.

On the normal course a student is involved for at least 20 per cent of his working week for a period ranging between three months and nine months, although some shorter block-release courses also exist. Naturally the longer the period, the more can be done – particularly as the integration of the educational and industrial elements is rarely instantaneous and to make progress towards an objective such as 'promoting individual personal development in and through the current changing work situation' is not easy.

One of the major curriculum devices used is the project and the principal one is usually centred around the students' workplace. Group projects are also used in which broad guide lines are given and the young people then are encouraged to organize their own work and activity from that basis. A structured feed-back is obtained in group seminars and students' experiences are shared as much as possible. In other words, although this is a reverse situation there are still some opportunities for participatory learning in good schemes and these possibilities are clearly underlined in the booklet of curriculum suggestions for organizers of schemes of Unified Vocational Preparation, revealingly entitled *Experience, Reflection, Learning* previously published by the Further Education Curriculum Review and Development Unit.

SOUTH DEVON TECHNICAL COLLEGE, UNIFIED VOCATIONAL
PREPARATION PROGRAMME
The South Devon U.V.P. programme involves 15 students for two-and-a-half days a week over a 10-week period. The College was invited by the D.E.S. to run a pilot scheme during the first year of the operation of U.V.P. The general aims are those of all such courses, namely, to assist students to assess their potential and to think realistically about their jobs and careers, to develop basic skills needed in adult life, to understand society and how it works, to strengthen skill and knowledge on which further education and training can be built.

The programme is based in college for two days and in employment for half a day, the remainder of the week being occupied by the student's normal job. The project directly relates the theoretical and practical sides of retail distribution from which area of employment students are drawn. The curriculum is devised jointly by employers, college staff and trade unions, to ensure practical realistic elements.

At the centre of the course is a project which each student completes, based upon the commodity group that the young person sells in his or her everyday job. This assignment and other questions relating to the programme involve the services of a mentor, normally the young person's immediate supervisor at work. They are further co-ordinated by visits from a college lecturer and a workbook is produced at the end of the programme.

Students are able to select their own field of study in the commodity project. They also organize activities during the residential element – e.g. a visit to London – which they wish to undertake. There is continual attention to the feedback from students as to the mix of curriculum and the areas to be studied.

As all participants on the programme are in full-time employment and following their normal occupations there is very close contact with industry at all times. Formally this is achieved through:

a. A participating employers working party;
b. Curriculum development working party;
c. Steering committee;
d. A mentor's briefing day;
e. Visits to mentors, managers and employees by college personnel.

Changes have been noted in the social behaviour of students such as an increase in confidence, motivation towards the job and motivation to undertake more training. There has also been a change in attitude of employers towards further education. These much more positive attitudes have been encouraged by the involvement of employers in curriculum design.

The use of experience at work as the core of the students' programme seems to be leading to particularly beneficial results.

9. *The Industrial Unit or Workshop approach*

An obvious development of work placement is for a college to create its own working unit in which the learning process is centred on, and stimulated by, a real production situation in which goods are made to order and then sold. In some projects of this kind there is an element of simulation, in that although there is a genuine cost-and-time pressure, the items are not actually sold but are broken down at the end of the process for the parts to be used again. This dilutes the reality of the project considerably and, since the majority of students are quite perceptive, must also limit its effectiveness. On the other hand there are a number of more thorough-going enterprises which do contain clear participatory elements.

Most such units face initial problems of financing and accommodation and even with local Authority goodwill and Manpower Service Commission's money it is not always easy for them to get off the ground. Another difficulty associated with producing goods for sale is that items have to be found which are not competing directly with local industry thus losing necessary goodwill and bringing opposition from trade unions because of possible lost jobs within the adult work force. These problems are always less acute if the student/employees are handicapped in some way but even with youngsters whose only disadvantage is an inability to gain employment an astute unit director can find acceptable products – very often they include specialist equipment for the education service which otherwise would not be produced.

The over-all organization of the students' programmes in the unit varies from the completely unstructured, where the teacher/supervisor deals with each youngster on an individual basis arising from his current work and personal experience, through some with a more formal input but still linked to the work of the unit through log books and projects, to the other extreme of allowing day-release to outside courses on an infill basis. The same range applies to student participation in the running of the unit with variations from benevolent dictatorship, usually with the handicapped, to attempts at total democracy. Even in the more authoritarian units, however, much effort goes into making the youngsters feel part of a team and giving them a sense of group responsibility but there is no doubt the major item of concern with this particular approach is to see that adherence to industrial reality does not sweep away the various indirect educational benefits which such a situation can create.

BRIDGEND COLLEGE, ADJUSTMENT TO INDUSTRY

This project aims to assist in the transition from school to work of less able school-leavers to give an assessment for work readiness and if necessary to provide a bridge between school, employment, further education and the adult training centre. Normally 30 young people are full-time student trainees who spend the whole of their week in a factory bought by the Mid-Glamorgan Education Committee which is situated on an industrial estate. The factory carries out contracts in wood, metal and light assembly products and all items produced are for sale. The tasks involved are deliberately different from school craft work and the students are given proper responsibilities rather than being left to carry out work of a demeaning nature which is so often the lot of this kind of young person in industry.

The factory is semi-autonomous in that it is quite isolated from the college. The students voluntarily accept the role of workers and each day a boy and girl are appointed chargehand and given proper responsibility. The students are not involved in over-all policy making however. The object is to provide a real working situation in which covert education arising from the jobs undertaken can continually take place. Detailed records are maintained and a fair amount of contact is kept with ex-students. Since September 1975 almost 100 less able students have been placed in employment and there has been a turnover of more than £20,000. There is a strong emphasis on the reality of the situation because the organizers believe that education for the handicapped should tail off to full-time work rather than involving them in an abrupt change. They also feel that exclusive concentration on reading and writing may be largely irrelevant to student needs and that for the youngsters involved this work is most successful when flowing directly from practical tasks in which they are involved. As with many of the developments described in this guide one of the greatest problems is the lack of suitable trained staff who can both impart knowledge of skills and also undertake the considerable counselling task which is necessary. Suitable staff are very important to such a venture if it is not to become a mere imitation of industry without the vital element of general personal development.

10.   *The Commercial Enterprise approach*

This is a more limited form of the workshop approach in production terms but one which has a wider involvement of students in all aspects of working together and of management. It is also an approach which can be made attractive to students of high academic ability because of the opportunities provided for demonstrating personal initiative. Although it contains elements of both production and business practice the value of such companies is in much more general areas such as problem solving, group spirit and individual responsibility.

In the United Kingdom many projects of this kind are run under the auspices of nationally-based non-profit making charitable organisations. The two best known are Young Enterprise and the Inter-Action Trust which both work within the same general structure of providing initial written information and visits from an Adviser but of allowing the group of students to make their own decisions from that point on as to what to make, how to make it, how to organize themselves and how to market their product.

The philosophies of the two promoting bodies do vary however. Whereas Young Enterprise lays more stress on the organizational side and on assistance with career choice and understanding industry, the Inter-Action scheme – known as Make it Yourself (M.I.Y.) – is described as a Community Education Experiment and there is an emphasis on benefiting others and on students learning the possibilities of self-help should they later become unemployed. This difference does not affect the stress on student participation, which is often of the order of 90 per cent or more in the running of the company, and these attempts which can involve more academic students in action projects are to be encouraged. From this point of view it is very helpful to have the publicity and selling power which the two national organizations possess and there seems every reason to believe that this kind of approach will be taken up by an increasing number of schools and colleges.

WALTON SCHOOL, STAFFORD, ODDIDOS LIMITED
This is a Young Enterprise company which has involved 25 sixth-form students throughout their first post 'O' level year. Significantly

the location was outside school at a local timber and joinery firm and the major objective of the exercise was simply to give the students an opportunity to run their own business.

The students formed their own company to produce a range of goods, money was raised by the sale of shares at 25p each, production lines were set up and finished goods were sold to parents, garden centres and department stores. In order to do this functions had to be divided up among the students and all the usual business decisions had to be taken regarding marketing, production and communications. The work took place immediately following afternoon school and at the end of the project an Annual General Meeting was called, a report and accounts were presented and a dividend was declared.

There was total student involvement in the running of the company and all final decisions were theirs although advisers were on hand from the host company to offer their assistance. Although there was no specific aim to co-ordinate this experience with the remainder of the student's 'A' level course, those studying Economics certainly found the background knowledge obtained to be useful. The students as a whole became more conscious of the problems and the challenges found by people working in industry through their experiences and this was particularly true of those who spent time on the management team. They learnt simply by doing, by having to handle other people, by having to take decisions, even with incomplete data, on situations which can occur in industry and by having to take responsibility for part of the firm's operations. It is interesting to note that Oddidos won the Company of the Year award presented by the B.B.C. T.V. programme *Nationwide*, in 1978. Much of the success of the venture was due to the interest aroused in the students and to the enthusiastic co-operation of the company whose premises they used.

11.   The Twinning approach

Another idea which is beginning to gain some favour in the United Kingdom as a way of causing a school to look outside its walls is that of twinning with an industrial concern. One spin-off from this twinning process is that students are often enabled to tackle live industrial problems and to work out their own answers to them as a group. A particularly successful example of this approach has been in Birmingham where for more than ten years a firm has provided problems for the students to solve. Though this is only simulation the students are enabled to compare their answers with those adopted by the firm thus giving some real-life dimension to their work.

One form of this approach which has Government backing is the Teaching Company, an arrangement sponsored in the Higher Education sector by the Science Research Council and the Department of Industry. The basic idea is for a twinning between a large company and a university or polytechnic that will produce an organization which can employ Industrial Associates to undertake actual research projects within the Company. The drive behind this is quite definitely one of vocational training (rather than of general development) and as such it is not experiential and participatory as defined in this study, but the concept is an interesting one and so closely related that it is worth recording.

BYNG KENRICK SCHOOL, BIRMINGHAM, GIRLING PROJECT

The Byng Kenrick School has had a close arrangement with the engineering firm of Girling Ltd. for a number of years. From the school side it involves a group of sixth-formers working on problems supplied by the company for an academic year. The intention is to give the students an idea of how industry works and some experience of industrial processes. The method is to present the group with live problems which they have to attempt to solve and then present their solution in written or model form after a period of about six weeks.

Each problem begins when the group visits the Girling Company and meets a senior executive, normally the production engineer. He speaks to them about some aspect of engineering and then takes them into the factory to show them a specific process, machine operation or materials test, relevant to the particular topic. They are then presented with a problem which they have to solve which usually involves the production of both drawings and hardware.

There is obviously little student involvement in the choice of project but they are entirely responsible for the final solution chosen for the problem presented to them and for the way in which that solution is displayed. The work of the group is often further disseminated into the school by having these solutions put on display.

This work has only been made possible by the enthusiastic co-operation of senior Girling staff. For the students possibly the most valuable part of the exercise is when they return to present their solution to the firm. They then evaluate it and compare it with the solution actually followed in practice. An important development of this kind of work would obviously be if the time-scale was such that not only was the problem live but also that the students' solution had some chance of being put into operation if it satisfactorily answered the needs of the practical situation.

Promotion of Learning by Participation

The need for further development and dissemination of ideas which are currently being practised in a relatively small number of locations is a recurring theme in this survey of the present study of learning by participation in the United Kingdom. Fortunately, as noted earlier, two attempts at what in the Netherlands could be called a stimulation strategy are now being promoted, one by the Further Education Curriculum Review and Development Unit (F.E.U.)[11] and the other by Community Service Volunteers (C.S.V.)[12].

The F.E.U. was first in the field with the publication in the Autumn, 1979, of a Register of Experiential and Participatory Learning and a Guide to Current Practice in this field, both being produced under the direction of Professor Gareth Williams, Director of the Instituute for Research and Development in Post-Compulsory Education at Lancaster University. The definition adopted in this work is parallel to that quoted in the first section although worded in a slightly different fashion. Projects for inclusion in the Register should ideally contain:

a. An element of 'real-life';
b. Student participation in the planning and/or operation of the project;
c. Proper integration of the 'real-life' element with the remainder of the students' school or college programmes.

Some 200 projects have been catalogued in such a way that their individual characteristics are clearly apparent and also that innovators in the field may get directly in touch with one another. There is indeed an element of the super-classified telephone directory about the publication, with entries presented on a single sheet in a ring binder format in the hope that the whole can be regularly up-dated.

The projects are classified under headings similar to the '11 approaches' method used here and these categories form the basis of the Guide to Current Practice published alongside the Register. The guide also draws out, and comments on, particular successes and problems experienced by practitioners. Its major purpose is not to lay down strict rules as to how participatory learning may best be achieved but rather to point to approaches which are working and encourage others to see which mode is most easily transferrable to their own situation.

Similar aims are behind C.S.V.'s Study Service enquiry, although this concentrates more on Higher Education and the 18—22 age-range whereas the work of the F.E.U. is mainly directed towards 15- to 19-year-olds, including both school and college programmes. There is some overlap between the two studies but fortunately they are, in the main, turning out to be complementary.

The C.S.V. enquiry resulted from a resolution at the 1976 UNESCO General Conference authorizing the Secretariat to undertake a fact-finding enquiry into the extent of Study Service, by which they principally meant ways in which the energies and abilities of students in Higher Education might be harnessed to assist in overcoming social problems. Alec Dickson, the Director of C.S.V., seized on this opportunity to persuade the Department of Education and Science to fund a two-year enquiry to see how the over-all concept of Study Service had existence and validity in the United Kingdom.

The definition used as a guide is that:

a. Students (not staff alone) should be involved;

b. Work should be an integral part of the curriculum – and preferably assessed;

c. There should normally be direct contact, at some stage at least of the course, between students and intended beneficiaries;

d. The effect of the work should be detectable at individual or small group level.

Much of this has an obvious relationship to Learning by Participation and it is hoped that the proposed case studies and the project report to the Department of Education and Science in 1980 will be powerful weapons to assist in its growth. As with the F.E.U.'s Register and Guide however, only interim reports have yet appeared but in both cases they seem to be encouraging in their findings with regard to the amounts of relevant projects now being operated.

Problems and Successes: Problems

In summarizing the current state of participatory and experiential learning in the United Kingdom it is first necessary to look at the difficulties being encountered by practitioners.

Acceptance

In the course of setting up a programme of participatory learning there are a number of groups and interests which have to be convinced. Firstly it is essential that staff and the institution are prepared to share their control of student learning, both with untrained outsiders and to some extent with the young people themselves. This is not an easy thing to do since it involves taking risks and accepting that no one group has a monopoly of wisdom.

In addition to gaining acceptance of staff such innovations may have to be sold to governing bodies and local education authorities if, as is likely, they bring with them requirements for resource allocation – particularly if they are for additional teaching hours. In the world outside education it may be necessary to seek trade union agreement, particularly for industrial placements, and it will certainly be essential to have the wholehearted support of employers whether in industry, in local or central government or in voluntary bodies. Indeed new venues for placement must be found when the level of support to the student is seen to be insufficient. One other factor which can affect acceptance of Learning by Participation programmes by all parties, but particularly by employers and by parents, is that they are quite likely to have no tangible results in the shape of examination passes or certificates, general development of the student being more difficult to demonstrate. This involves the problem of evaluation, which will be mentioned separately on p. 127.

Organization

In terms of the organization of an institution there are a number of points which must be sorted out if experiential and participatory learning is to work in a particular location. The first of these is the relatively straightforward matter of timetabling. This includes both the length of time given to such work, so that it does not reduce too greatly the time for more academic studies, and its arrangement, in that blocks somewhat lengthier than normal have to be provided for external experience to be worthwhile. An initial solution to both questions where they are a cause of difficulty can be found by allowing the out-of-college element to take place, at least partly, out of normal college hours. The combination of learning centred on projects, surveys or placements, which may begin to create its own demands on time, energy and interest, with the more formal needs of a course such as preparation for an external examination, can cause tension. This problem is likely to become more extreme with students on courses which have a greater academic content until eventually formal learning takes over and the gaining of experience is delegated entirely to outside bodies. Such bodies are often admirable but they cannot properly help to ensure that what is learnt in class is seen to have a relationship with life outside school or college. There is a place for this vital task within the minority time of the most demanding course for 16- to 19-year-olds, to underline the fact that education is, in part at least, a preparation for life.

The major organizational and curriculum problem associated with participatory learning is of course to see that the increasing use of external experience is properly linked with learning within the institution. Too often in the past the experience has been regarded as an end in itself but this is not enough for an educational enterprise. A combination of journals, discussion sessions, assignments, individual tutorials and other methods whose content is based on the out of college work is needed. Ensuring that this takes place and that the two elements, internal and external, do not drift apart is an essential duty for course organizers and it is with such matters that the outside viewpoint, provided, for instance, by the role of the education worker in the social education approach, can be so important.

Placement

As has been suggested above, finding a placement where the employers are sufficiently supportive can be a problem. In addition to this it must be recognized that an increase in work of this kind, while it can add to the resources available to education, is bound to lead to a situation in which new placements become hard to find simply because of the number of demands made. Saturation point is still a long way off in terms of the possibilities available but as more locations are used up more time will be needed to recruit a wider base of support. This does not imply however that these methods lose greatly in cost-effectiveness since the placements generated can represent a great saving in staff time as compared with courses taught completely by more formal methods.

The amount of support which young people receive from their employers and supervisors on placement depends to some extent on the philosophy adopted by the firm or organization. If placements are seen merely as a form of substitute work or cheap labour then their educational value, pariicularly that derived from participation, will be lost. The usefulness of placements can also be destroyed by much more simple practical things such as the availability of transport. It is no use offering a group of disadvantaged youngsters the most splendid opportunity for a project if it is miles out in the country and lacking in a suitable bus service.

Spread of Opportunity

Although ideally learning by participation should be available in some form to all young people there are associated difficulties in achieving this end. The first of these is the fact that so much attention is being paid to the unemployed and the disadvantaged, particularly through schemes begun under the Youth Opportunities Programme, that it makes it appear that such learning is designed only for the system's rejects. This seems to be a problem common to each country in this study. As has been said previously this tendency can be exaggerated by the apparently greater difficulty of combining less formal work with the remainder of the programme of students studying for examinations. The tendency to use these methods with young people who have experienced difficulties can also give problems to the teachers, in that a group can contain students suffering from environmental disadvantage, ethnic disadvantage and personal backwardness – on occasions from all three at once. This can obviously throw great strain on the staff, an effect not always recognized by those who assess the relative importance of courses.

Staffing

Finding the right staff is essential and the problem hinted at in the preceding paragraph, that in terms of the Burnham Report on the grading of courses[14] this work does not generate posts other than at the basic level, is a stumbling block to growth. This is also seen in other areas of work in further education, but given the difficulties of developing participatory learning properly then it is asking staff to show undue devotion to tackle them with no great hope of future reward. It is also true that staff are involved in work of this kind because of their own enthusiasm for it rather than because they have received any kind of relevant training. This may be fine for pioneering, but in extension and consolidation something more is required in the way of preparation.

Successes

Having explored the immediate problems associated with the introduction of Learning by Participation it is essential to balance them by some reference to the ways in which this work seems to be beginning to achieve some success. Many of the schemes are quite new and any claims must therefore of necessity be tentative.

Personal Skills

With students on courses at all levels the general reinforcing value of experience is noted. An active role in carrying out a task seems to impress itself more on the mind than the more passive role of the learner in the classroom. In personal terms this is generally expressed as a noticeable improvement in confidence, in general manner and maturity. For many of the young people involved the fact that they are a necessary part of a project and prove to be effective in their involvement can give them a sense of their own worth which has previously been lacking. This apparent ability to build up, not the expectations of young people, but their readiness to see themselves facing up to problems and challenges can be one of the most helpful aspects of this work.

A number of respondents to the F.E.U. project mentioned the way in which the attraction of a new interest can lead students into improvements in their basic skills of literacy and numeracy; the discovery that these skills are a vital necessity if they are to write for jobs or take measurements in relation to the project with which they are involved seems to come to many young people as a surprise. It has often been the experience in further education that staff have found that some students need to see a direct outcome before they can appreciate the value of formal learning. This can form another facet of that giving of self-respect noted in the preceding paragraph.

Social Skills

Under this heading two beneficial effects are recorded. Firstly there is the value of group work in completing some co-operative enterprise. Young people learn to work with each other and to make allowances for personal difficulties within the group. They can also of course, depending on the nature of the programme, learn how to handle others including members of the general public.

Many programmes also demonstrate the way in which young people can make a genuine contribution to society. This is certainly a factor which can help to increase the appeal of education itself to the public at large.

Vocational Appreciation

Although participatory learning is directed principally towards extending the general education of young people and is not involved in teaching specific vocational skills as a major aim, there are obvious spin-offs from many of these programmes in the field of preparation for work. The increase in personal and social skills noted above can help students, and particularly those who are disadvantaged, to compete more successfully for employment. It is true that the interest aroused and the confidence gained from participating in this kind of programme can increase students' interest both in work and in further training.

.This access aspect of Learning by Participation in which it may assist in re-directing young people towards worthwhile jobs and re-entry to some pattern of education is an area which seems to be proving successful. This can also be true in a slightly different way for students on more academic courses who may have their eyes opened to aspects of working life and of managerial roles which would not otherwise have been offered to them. As so many of these students sooner or later become managers in commerce or industry this again is a helpful by-product of this kind of programme.

Liaison

In more general areas schemes involving participatory learning can help in successful liaison between educational institutions and outside bodies. The fact that many programmes have useful outcomes can in itself be a valuable public relations factor and create a receptive attitude towards the college or school. Links can be strengthened with parents because a new idea has to be properly explained to them.

The most important relationship is usually that with the various employers involved whether public, private or voluntary. The difficulties have been noted previously, but handled correctly there can also be great gains. Where employers are fully involved in a scheme both by contributing to its planning and by offering interested supervsion, then their attitude to education can be greatly changed. This change can be enormously reinforced by the general performance of the young people placed with a particular employer. The relationship between workplace and educational institution can be made to work well for both parties if proper efforts are made to see that communications between them are constructive and well maintained.

The Institution

Apart from the excitement of breaking relatively new ground for a particular school or college, institutions mainly benefit from the involvement and development of staff. Programmes of participatory learning always require that staff shall innovate in their work and the sometimes delicate task of directing a project without too openly appearing to do so can be very beneficial for the individual concerned. Also those schemes which demand a team approach can help in breaking down the isolationist attitude of some staff.

Staff development of this kind needs related training to be properly effective and so from the emerging successes of the present we must turn to the requirements of the future.

The Future of Learning by Participation in the United Kingdom

What has been described in this chapter is not a formally devised curriculum or even an agreed attitude to it but rather an emergence in different parts of the United Kingdom of locally inspired schemes which appear to have certain basic criteria in common. These criteria also seem to answer some of the needs currently requiring the attention of the education service, and if these needs are to continue to be met in this way then as a start the following general developments could well be initiated.

The Need for Staff Training

If there is to be any long term development of Learning by Participation and if it is to be properly applied in the United Kingdom then it must begin to be understood by those who train teachers and some element of preparation for this kind of work should be inserted into pre-service courses where possible. There are already one or two colleges which promote general community awareness in their students and there are clear examples of this in the work of the R.O.S.L.A. Unit in Bristol and at Hoyland Hall.

Some of this work was highlighted at a conference on 'Preparation for Teaching in Urban Areas' organized by the Centre for Educational Disadvantage[15] in December, 1978. At this conference it was stated that young student teachers need new kinds of preparation for teaching in Inner City Schools, in particular community placements which allow for sustained local contact so that the students were not seen as temporary intruders. Participatory learning is not only valuable in an urban context, of course, but the tone of this conference and the foundation of a working party to further its ideas have made a useful platform for closely related improvements within the world of teacher training. It would now be helpful if a group could be formed of those interested in experiential and participatory learning, particularly within the technical teacher-training colleges, to promote its inclusion in the training of those most likely to have to make innovations with young people in this way.

The Need for Evaluation

If people are to be persuaded to put time and money into the growth of learning by participation then some acceptable form of project evaluation needs to be developed. Evaluation is a very delicate matter since, although it is possible to chart improvements in numeracy and literacy or the percentage of students who obtain jobs, this is not really what experiential and participatory learning is about. The important matters are intangibles such as improvement in self-confidence or sensitivity to others for which it is virtually impossible to construct a standard mechanical test. Indeed among some course or project directors there is positive antagonism to the individual evaluation of students on grounds ranging from the danger of destroying the essentially co-operative relationship neces-sary between staff and young people, to the feeling that it would be wrong to create a situation in which someone could be said to fail in 'life-skills' and hence in life itself. Great faith is placed in empiricism and as one person said in response to a question on arrangements for evaluation on the Further Education Unit questionnaire, 'none had been made since if it has no value it will die of natural causes'.

Somehow, however, if participatory learning is to have validity for uncommitted people an acceptable method of evaluation will have to be found which avoids on the one hand the blanket refusal to go beyond gut feeling as expressed in the previous statement, and on the other cries for pinning innovation down under the weight of a critical path analysis or some similarly complex process. It may be that a simple form of profile on which improvements in relevant qualities are graded on a 5 or 6 point scale is as far as anyone dare tread along this road – but what is certain is that it must be explored.

If local schemes are to be nationally validated then it will be necessary for an agreed form of evaluation to be developed and it is hoped that the Further Education Unit may be able to act as a catalyst in this process.

In the United Kingdom there is a great danger of a large percentage of our young people suffering from alienation and boredom. Programmes which channel teenagers' energies into education through their involvement in useful experiences are too valuable a life-line to be lightly dismissed. There is of course another danger in all this; once young people become actively and responsibly involved, they may wish to go on participating and to have an increased say in their adult lives. Surely however this is a risk worth taking and the introduction of Learning by Participation could have positive results far beyond those of merely making people more employable.

Notes and References

1. The Newsom Report *Half our Future*.
   A report of the Central Advisory Council for Education presented by its Chairman, Mr. John Newsom, in August, 1963. The terms of reference were for the Council to advise the Ministry of Education on the education of pupils aged 13—16 of average or less than average ability.
2. R.O.S.L.A.
   The school-leaving age was raised from 15 to 16 during the academic year 1972—3. This meant that there were no 15-year-old leavers in July, 1972. The process was popularly known as R.O.S.L.A.
3. The Schools Council.
   The Schools Council was set up in October, 1964 by the Ministry of Education to carry out research and development work on curricula, teaching methods and examinations in primary and secondary schools. It is an independent body representing all sectors of the education field with school teachers forming a majority of its members. One of its main objectives is 'to uphold and interpret the principle that each school should have the fullest possible measure of responsibility for its own work with its own curriculum and teaching methods based on the needs of its own pupils and evolved by its own staff'.

4. City and Guilds.
   The City and Guilds of London Institute (C.G.L.I.) was founded in 1878 and has since become the major examining body for non-advanced technical and vocational courses in the United Kingdom. It offers a wide range of subjects numbering about 300 in all, of which Engineering, Technology and Applied Science are the most popular.
5. Open College.
   The Open College concept is for re-entry courses for adults who have been out of formal education for some considerable time. Their distinguishing characteristics are that they are made up of a number of free-standing units which can be combined to form courses in a flexible fashion and that methods of study, including 'Distance-Study', are related to adult needs and a student can easily drop out and then return again before completing the whole course. Currently these opportunities are available in the North West of England, in the North East, the Midlands and Inner London.
6. Cambridgeshire Village Colleges.
   In the 1930s Henry Morris, the Secretary for Education in Cambridgeshire, put forward a scheme for Village Colleges where primary, secondary, adult and part-time vocational education could all be carried on side by side. The intention was to provide eleven such colleges to be community centres for their neighbourhood where 'a child would enter at three and leave the college only in extreme old age'. Four were opened before the 1939—45 war at Sawston, Bottisham, Linton and Impington, and have continued to exert a powerful influence on the thought of innovative educators in the United Kingdom.
7. The Manpower Services Commission.
   The Manpower Services Commission (M.S.C.) was established in 1974 by the Employment and Training Act of 1973. It is responsible for the whole of the Employment and Training Services of the Government, and works through two major sections, the Employment Services Division and the Training Services Division.
8. E.S.N.(M.)
   E.S.N. stands for Educationally Sub-normal (Medium). Educationally sub-normal children were defined for the first time in the United Kingdom, in 1945, as those whose learning capacities were so poor as to warrant special provision apart from the main stream of schools. The definition is educational rather than medical. Special schools for these children are now divided into two groups, that is for those just below an acceptable level for normal schooling, E.S.N.(M.), and the severely sub-normal, E.S.N.(S.).
10. *A Better Start in Working Life.*
   A consultative paper presented jointly by the Departments of Employment and Education, published in 1978. It outlines proposals for extending the provision made for those young people who enter jobs where little or no systematic training or further education is provided.

11.   The Further Education Curriculum Review and Development Unit (F.E.U.).
An advisory, intelligence and development body for further education. It was established in 1977 by the Secretary of State for Education and Science to make possible a more co-ordinated and cohesive approach to curriculum development in F.E. by:
1. reviewing the range of existing curricula and identifying overlap, duplication and deficiencies;
2. determining priorities for action to improve the total provision and suggesting ways in which improvement can be effected;
3. carrying out specific studies, helping with curricular experiments and contributing to the evaluation of objectives;
4. disseminating information about the process of curriculum development in F.E.

12.   Community Service Volunteers (C.S.V.).
A voluntary organization funded by the Voluntary Services Unit of the Home Office. Its principal objective is to involve young people in community service and to encourage social change. It does this through five major programmes:
a full-time volunteer programme which places over 2,000 young people a year;
an advisory service which provides ideas and materials for schools and colleges wishing to involve pupils and students in service related to the curriculum;
a programme for disadvantaged volunteers, borstal trainees and children in care;
a media programme which works with the Independent Broadcasting Authority and commercial radio and T.V. companies to recruit volunteers;
a youth employment programme which operates a number of youth opportunities schemes in different parts of the country, involving over a thousand young people.

13.   Burnham Report on the Grading of Courses.
The Burnham Further Education Report lays down the salary scales for all teaching staff in colleges. The basis on which Local Education Authorities consider the grading of full-time posts is related to the quantity of work but also to the category within which different courses fall. The allocation of courses to the different grades of work is published in the Grading of Courses booklet which has to be read in conjunction with the current Burnham Report. Courses such as those referred to in this chapter are all in the lowest grade, thus carrying least reward for the staff involved.

14.   The Centre for Educational Disadvantage.
The Centre, for information and advice on educational disadvantage, was set up by the Department of Education and Science in Manchester during 1976 and is to be closed during 1980 as part of the Government economy measures. Its work has fallen broadly into four categories – for ethnic minorities, women and girls, under-achievers,

and special-school-leavers, particularly those designated educationally sub-normal.

CHAPTER FOUR
The United States

BRUCE DOLLAR

In comparison with most European educational systems, that of the United States is highly decentralized and shows marked openness. As a consequence of this, thousands of programmes incorporating LBP principles run because of local initiative, and many have been documented by the National Commission on Resources for Youth (NCRY). Although the absence of a national educational system means that the US federal government has no direct authority over schools, it does influence school practice by providing funds for special programmes, and has sponsored several major LBP programmes for young people. Bruce Dollar describes these efforts at both the local and federal levels in the following chapter. Mr Dollar was until recently Associate Director of NCRY.

Learning experiences that take place outside school walls have attracted much sympathetic attention in the United States in recent years. Since a series of influential study commissions issued reports during the early 1970s calling for more 'real world' experiences for young people, educational policy makers have sought increasingly to introduce participation learning into programmes for youth. Government-sponsored learning programmes now often incorporate youth participation into their design, while older, more traditional programmes like vocational education are being modified to include it. At the local level, meanwhile, hundreds of programmes employing Learning by Participation have been created to meet immediately felt needs of youth, school and community.

This avid interest in out-of-school learning is less a new idea than the revival of an old one. Its currency, in fact, is a reaction to a more recent, modern notion: that formal, school-bound learning can adequately prepare the young to take their place in society as adults. Previously, this preparation had been accomplished through a variety of informal means, including the family, the neighbourhood, and religion. When industrialization and modernization disrupted these traditional institutions, however, schools were deliberately developed to assume their socializing functions. Then, as formal education spread and consolidated itself into a system, these informal institutions of learning shrank in significance. 'Education' came to mean what took place in schools, and today the schools are vested with the primary responsibility for preparing the young for adulthood.

Americans have always harboured a romantic mythology about public education. In the popular mind, historically the schools have served as the great engine of social assimilation for a diverse immigrant population. The schools, it was thought, could overcome the disadvantages of class, nationality, race and other accidents of birth, transforming scarcely civilized children into responsible, productive citizens. As a means of dealing with modernization, the schools could provide the rigorous formal education required by industrialization and technology, teaching skills for the future that were no longer within the capacity of traditional training methods such as the apprenticeship system. Schools were also valued because they isolated the young from society, providing a protected environment that was needed for serious study and a haven from a hostile, unjust world.

At the same time as they were ostensibly serving these functions, however, schools were also responding to changing economic realities in ways that reinforced and expanded their role as society's chief socializing institution for the young. When compulsory school attendance and anti-child-labour laws were passed – with the enthusiastic support of labour interests – one effect was to remove children from competition for jobs. As technology advanced, the number of unskilled jobs declined and more complex skills were needed to fill the jobs of the future. The period of school attendance was extended accordingly, until a high school diploma was considered minimal certification to get a decent job. American educators congratulate themselves on having achieved universal secondary education, with over 90 per cent of today's adolescent population in high school compared with scarcely 10 per cent in 1900. Many young people, of course, continue their formal schooling uninterrupted well into their twenties. Young people who once were economically productive members of their families and society are today financially either burdens or luxuries for many families, and economically significant to society mainly as consumers.

In the 1960s many traditional attitudes and beliefs about schools began to be seriously challenged. An awareness grew of the schools' role in reproducing the social structure, reinforcing and legitimizing class and racial differences rather than diminishing them. Formal education that was limited to a one-way transfer of subject matter from teacher to student was attacked as lifeless and boring. And the segregation of school-bound young people from the real world of adults was seen as denying them the experiences they needed to be adequately prepared for adulthood. Even the schools' function of equalizing economic opportunity was thrown into question. The inevitable consequence of universal secondary education and greatly expanded post-secondary education was to reduce the value of both high school diplomas and college degrees. Rises in all levels of both unemployment and educational costs prompted urgent questions about the value of formal schooling. And two widely publicized research studies found that schools had little differential impact on either academic achievement or adult success.[1]

Young people themselves played an important role in bringing about the reassessment of American schools during the 1960s. The civil rights, anti-war and ecology movements, in which youth figured prominently, abetted a widespread disaffection toward established institutions, with much of youth's alienation naturally directed against the schools. The mood of political activism and assertion of individual rights clashed head-on with the schools' insistence on keeping students passive and dependent. Young people were demanding subject matter that was 'more relevant' to their lives as well as more control over their lives, both in and out of school. Many viewed young people's apparent rejection of society as one part of an alarming youth pathology that included drug abuse, increasing crime rate and school vandalism and violence, perhaps failing to realize that young people themselves felt society had already rejected them, consigning them to uselessness in 'youth ghettos' (schools).

Beginning in the early 1970s a succession of government and professional study commissions were formed to seek explanations for the 'youth crisis'. With unusual unanimity, their reports[2] both challenged deeply held assumptions about education and criticized the way society, particularly its schools, prepares youth for adulthood. The exclusion of youth from the activities of the adult world, it was observed, takes place in an era in which young people have more of the physical and mental tools for participation than ever before. Physical maturity occurs increasingly earlier – two years earlier today than at the turn of the century. And modern communications media assure a steady stream of information. Whereas a century ago the young, as one report put it, were 'action-rich' and 'information-poor', today that situation has been reversed. Schools are maintained as 'aging vats' that force passivity, prolong dependence, and delay the learning of adult roles, work habits and skills. The effect is to block the opportunity of young people to fulfil some of their most urgent needs: to develop, through interaction with the real world, a sense of individual identity and self-worth; and to develop, through mutually responsible and mutually rewarding involvement with others, a capacity for social maturity. The reports called for a concerted effort to reintegrate the young into adult society by broadening conceptions of what constitutes education, by forging cooperative links between schools and communities and workplaces, and by experimenting with learning programmes that enable the young to participate actively in their own education and in the adult world.

While changes of the sort these reports recommended face formidable institutional and societal barriers, the reports did influence central authorities to seek ways of introducing Learning by Participation into government-sponsored programmes. Meanwhile, virtually ignored by all this discussion and planning at the top, a great deal of innovative activity was already taking place in local communities. The same social ferment that prompted the top-level studies had already spawned thousands of programmes at the local level which aimed precisely at providing participatory roles for young people.[3] In 1979, a national survey of high school community service programmes revealed for the first time the scope of this local movement as it affected the nation's public and private high schools, approximately 22,000 of them. Conducted by the National Center for Service-Learning, the study found that 92 per cent of all high schools in the United States offer students opportunities to address social and environmental problems in their own local communities. Focusing only on those programmes that were integrated into the curriculum in some way, the study also found the following:

1. Nationally, 14 per cent of all high schools – public and private – have curriculum-related service programmes.

2. These curriculum-related programmes have an average of 119 students actively involved, giving a total of some 336,000 students on a national basis.
3. Nearly two thirds of all curriculum-related programmes (64 per cent) award academic credit to the students. About half of these extend credit for classwork which is required as a part of the service programme; the other half extend credit for the service work itself.
4. The trend toward credit is relatively new: more than two-thirds of all schools awarding credit for service work (67 per cent) have begun doing so since 1974.
5. High school students involved in service-learning programmes put in an average of five hours a week in their communities, and another three hours in related classwork.
6. If the value of this work in the community is calculated at the minimum wage, the average school programme entails approximately $1,500-worth of student service work a week, or $55,000-worth in an academic year.
7. Students are most apt to be involved in programmes involving health services, tutoring, and companionship activities. Other activities frequently cited include ecology, pre-school and day care activities, and recreation programmes.[4]

How is it possible that so many innovative programmes were able to take root in local schools and communities unbeknown to central authorities? Part of the answer lies in a natural inability of planners and reformers at the national level to recognize solutions they have not discovered or prescribed themselves. To account for the local invention itself, one has to look at the way the American education system is organized.

Public schooling in the United States is highly decentralized. Although legally they are under the jurisdiction of the various state governments, schools are really controlled locally, where district boards of education set policies and from where the majority of financing emanates. When the teachers of a school district go on strike, for instance (as they are doing with growing frequency), it is against their local board of education. While it is true that this system of local control has contributed to much conservatism in educational and fiscal matters, it has also ensured enough slack over all to permit numerous pockets where innovative approaches may be tried – much more so, apparently, than in countries where school practices are centrally controlled.

The federal (national) government has no direct authority over schooling in the United States. Federal policy makers nonetheless have mounted major efforts over the past 20 years to influence school practice to meet nationally-defined needs such as improved education for minorities and poor children. Lacking the power to force compliance with its education policies, the federal government must rely on positive incentives (chiefly money), and persuasion, to win acceptance by state and local systems.

Federal attempts to promote central programme goals take two forms. One is to contract with a research and development institution to design a programme according to federal specifications that will be suitable for adoption by local systems. A second approach is to announce federal programme goals generally and to invite local systems to design their own programmes which will be eligible for federal support money. Sometimes both strategies are employed to promote the same innovation, as in the case of career education. The federal government has both sponsored its own model career education programmes (one of which is described below) and provided funds for locally developed programmes.

There are more than 16,000 independent public school districts across the United States, creating a vast potential for innovative activity, even though much of it may be small-scale and obscure. Coupled with federally-sponsored development of new programmes, and a climate which for a time seemed very hospitable to educational alternatives, this has produced an extraordinary (when compared to most other countries) interest and involvement in innovation. Indeed, so pervasive was the preoccupation with innovation from the mid-1960s to the mid-1970s that the last several years have seen a reaction in the form of a 'back to basics' movement which seeks to eliminate the 'frills' that presumably attach to departures from traditional schooling. This reaction has been reinforced, if not prompted, by the continuing economic squeeze. The resulting mood of relative austerity has somewhat curtailed innovation, both centrally and locally originated.

Innovative programmes employing LBP principles have originated in both local schools and communities and resulted from federal policy initiatives. As unique products of their own environment, local programmes tend to be well adapted to their specific local settings. Developed individually and independently, they are idiosyncratic and extremely diverse, but often poorly documented and not easily transferred to other settings. Federal attempts to introduce new educational programmes into local systems often involve well designed, fully developed programme models intended to work in many settings. Based on the latest research, thoroughly tested and documented, and supported by extensive resource materials, these programmes are a source of ideas and experience for everyone. As 'imported' products, however, they often meet resistance from local practitioners who do not share the priorities of central planners. While locally developed programmes are 'owned' by the people who take part in them, externally developed programmes must be 'sold' to these same people. Much has been learned from these costly federal attempts to induce local acceptance of imported programmes. Experience has shown that participation in the development of an alternative programme is a key factor in its successful implementation[5] – a finding that will come as no surprise to those who are already acquainted with the power of participation as a force for engagement and motivation. In more recent years, a trend toward more federal sponsorship of locally developed programmes has caused the line between central and local programmes to become less distinct.

Locally Developed LBP Programmes

Locally originating programmes of participation have been developed in sufficient numbers to qualify as a movement of sorts. Unlike some previous educational innovations that have been devised externally and then promulgated to the school system as the latest reform, however, Learning by Participation has been very much a grass-roots movement. Rather than a response to educational reformers who have defined the need and the solution, these programmes have been the product of local or individual responses to a locally- or individually-felt need. They have been a practitioner's, rather than a theorist's or planner's response; that is, they have been designed and operated for the most part by teachers and, in many cases, by students themselves. Many projects that have sprung up outside the schools have followed a similar pattern, having been set up by concerned individuals who saw a way to bring their own interests and skills together with the needs of a group of young people.

One very well known programme, called *Foxfire*, is a perfect example of this unique match of community conditions, youth resources and needs, and catalyzing adult leader. It began in the Southern Appalachian town of Rabun Gap, Georgia, when a class of high school students and their teacher both got bored with the regular curricular materials and began looking for an alternative. They hit upon the idea of documenting the folk wisdom of the old mountain people in their area and reporting it in their own magazine, which they named *Foxfire*. The result over the last few years has been the rescue of a priceless cultural heritage of crafts, folkways and reminiscences that might have died unrecorded with the last generation that carried it in their heads but for the efforts of the young people of *Foxfire*. So rich was their source that the material printed in this magazine has been collected into six books, each of which in turn has become a national bestseller.[6]

Because these local programmes were developed idiosyncratically to meet unique sets of local conditions, they are extraordinarily diverse, making it difficult to classify them or generalize about them. Fortunately, there is an organization, the National Commission on Resources for Youth, that has devoted its activities precisely to monitoring and learning from these local efforts. Founded in 1967 for the express purpose of promoting opportunities for young people to assume responsible roles in society, NCRY has elaborated its own definition of youth participation which it uses as a guide for classifying local projects that come to its attention. According to the definition, Youth Participation programmes:

> involve youth in responsible, challenging action, that meets genuine needs, with opportunity for planning and/or decision-making affecting others, in an activity whose impact or consequences extends to others – i.e. outside or beyond the youth participants themselves.

Other features are 'provision for critical reflection on the participatory activity and the opportunity for a group effort toward a common goal.'[7] This definition is not an official prescription which new programmes must follow. Rather it is a description of an ideal programme which NCRY, a youth-advocacy organization, uses as a standard against which actual programmes may be compared.

Local programmes are often created when a need is identified in a community which young people can help meet. Since communities all have many unmet needs, and since the young are capable of a great deal, the range of possibilities for worthwhile LBP activities seems virtually limitless. Indeed, because local programmes by and large have not been developed according to a generalized plan, they take a wide variety of forms. They vary, for example, as to programme structure, type of activity, institutional setting, size, clientele, and so forth. The National Commission on Resources for Youth classifies programmes geographically and by content area. The following partial listing of categories should give an idea of their range:

Communications and the Arts
    film, TV, radio, video
    journalism
    theatre arts
    visual arts
Community Fieldwork and Action
    community research
    archeology and historical preservation
    consumer services
    housing action
    museums and libraries
    the elderly
    recreation
Health Care
    physical health
    mental health
    mental retardation
    health information and referral
Problem Solving
    peer counseling
    drug and alcohol rehabilitation
    race relations
    policy advisement
    residential co-ops
Educational Services
    curriculum development
    early child care
    tutoring and teaching

Problems of Minorities
  Black
  Hispanic
  other ethnic groups
  women
Ecology and the Environment
  Construction and Restoration
Employment and Entrepreneurship
  business
  employment bureau
Legal Counselling, Information and Action
  Youth Advocacy
School Governance

It should perhaps be stressed that youth participants in programmes in these categories are not receivers but rather *providers* of
the services and actions indicated on the list.

As this categorization was derived while classifying actual
programmes brought to the attention of NCRY, it shows the wide
range of activities to which Learning by Participation may be
applied. LBP is similarly versatile in its possible relationships with
different institutional settings. Programmes have been started by
teachers or other school personnel, by community youth-serving
agencies, by independent or non-affiliated adults, and by young
people themselves, either in their capacity as students or as
community youth. They have been based in specialized youth-
serving institutions like houses for runaways and juvenile detention
facilities. Even within these institutions there is room for great
diversity. A school-connected LBP programme, for example, may
be one of the following:

a. a class in its own right, with credit;
b. a unit within an established course (e.g., a full-time project of
   limited duration or one that takes up a portion of weekly class
   time);
c. a free-period or off-hours project, either for credit or not;
d. cooperative arrangement: project operated jointly by a person
   from the school and a person from the community;
e. an outside agency operates the programme inside a school;
f. an outside agency operates the programme in the community,
   students get school credit.

The following section provides brief descriptions of programme types. Based mostly on programmes in NCRY files, they illustrate the many forms of LBP that NCRY has documented.[8] The headings under which they are presented, which focus on the programme activity, are neither exact nor complete. Many programmes fit none of them precisely; some programmes fit more than one. Nevertheless, the descriptions do provide some concrete illustrations while once again indicating the range of programme possibilities.

Helping service to others.

Young participants in these programmes meet regularly and face to face with other people in a helping relationship. Such others may be infants and pre-school children, elementary school children, retarded or handicapped children or adults, age peers, hospital patients, or old people. It is usual for participants to travel several times a week to the institution (day-care centre, elementary school, hospital, home for the aged, etc.) that serves the people to be helped. Concurrently, they carry on experience-based study of the related field – early childhood development, health services, the aged in society, etc. While these programmes deal in service to others, they are noteworthy for their benefits to the young people themselves, who often gain dramatically in self-esteem, responsibility and other dimensions.

Social action.

These are usually group projects in which the energies of a group of young people are directed toward achieving some social benefit or change. A project may begin with the identification of a problem facing the community or a segment of it, followed by an investigation of possible solutions, and culminating in the action decided upon. Each step in this process involves participation by the group. Some examples are a consumer-action service in which young people invite consumer complaints which they try to rectify by dealing with the offending company; a project in which urban youth locate and report housing law violations to city authorities; the establishment and operation of a food-buying cooperative for poor people.

Community construction.

In one programme, young people provide emergency repairs to the houses of aging or handicapped poor people at no cost to the homeowner. In another, high school students design, build and renovate houses as part of an urban redevelopment plan. In a third type of construction programme, students restore dilapidated historic buildings in their town. A 150-year-old church, for example, was restored and converted to a community arts centre. Students' entire curriculum relates to their community experience, including construction mathematics, local history, science and English.

Community archaeology.

These projects usually begin when someone discovers traces of ancient life in the community, often on school property. Under the supervision of an archeologist, students unearth pottery fragments, stone tools, bones, and so forth, while learning geography, history, anthropology and ecology. The project may become a class in the school curriculum. In a variation of this type of project, a resident of a historic town organized local youth to restore a neglected colonial-era cemetery. In addition to manual labour, the young people did research and historical documentation, and eventually the local high school agreed to grant academic credit for this work. Later, students in this project travelled throughout their state telling other young people what they had learned and training them to do similar projects in their own towns.

Communications and the arts.

In a New York City project, young people have learned art principles and skills by participating in making public works of art such as murals or outdoor sculptures for their neighbourhoods. Under the supervision of professional artists, youths take part in the entire project from conception through execution, often receiving high school credit. Other projects involve young people in conducting interviews and research in their communities and printing their results in a community magazine. In one exemplary project, high school students produced professional-quality videotapes to inform the public and influence decisions on important municipal issues. The video-tapes are done as a service to community agencies – such as a tenants' rights organization or a community health clinic – which request the tapes for use in educating their clinetele. Students receive academic credit in social studies.

Ecology.

In many of these programmes students do work such as beach conservation, or aluminium recycling, while studying the environment. Many others involve action to defend the environment. One science-based project documented the pollution of a river scientifically and brought successful legal action against the culprit. Another organized public sentiment in a lobbying effort to pass a law to protect endangered wildlife in the area. Students in these projects also designed ecology lessons and taught them to elementary school children.

Services to peers.

Several different types of peer counselling programmes have emerged in which young people help each other understand and cope with their feelings and concerns by learning some simple listening and counselling skills. Both individual and group counselling approaches have been successful. Projects sometimes concentrate on specific problems such as drug abuse. Another kind of peer service is a career centre in which young people are trained and either paid, or given school credit, to help other students on employment matters, including job-seeking skills, information and job placement.

Internships.

This is quite a common form of LBP programme in which young people are placed individually with adults at their work place in the community. The 'interns' are each given their own responsibilities while they also learn about the work of the mentor or 'community teacher'. The interns may all meet in a class or 'seminar' to discuss what they are learning or they may develop individual learning contracts or do their own community projects in conjunction with their placement. In a project in which all young people are interns in community service agencies, a curriculum can be developed, based on related issues and practices. Naturally, the more diverse the community placements the more difficult it is to devise a common curriculum.

Health and medical.

In a cooperative arrangement with a university hospital, high school students in one programme spend one day a week working with medical personnel, including physicians, technicians, researchers and therapists. A condition of their placement is that they do actual work such as research or physical therapy. They also have a weekly seminar taught at the hospital by medical professionals and students, as well as an academic class curriculum based on their experience. In another project, young people are trained as 'health consultants' to counsel their peers in dealing with health-related problems of adolescence.

Entrepreneurship.

When a budget-cut eliminated a school's hot lunch programme, the students organized themselves to operate their own. They now do all menu planning, food ordering, cooking and cleaning for a daily meal for the school, earning enough money to pay for their operation, including wages for two trained adults. The school incorporated the activity as a commercial cooking course, and recently the programme expanded to bread baking, with profitable sales in the community. In a community-based project, young people created and maintained a natural science museum which provides education and recreation for themselves, younger children, and the rest of the community. High school students in another project formed a student-controlled credit union that helped students secure loans and save over $41,000 in six years.

University-based programmes.

Colleges and universities have sponsored quite a range of programmes that allow students to learn by participation. One form of programme is community-action research, in which students ask community organizations to identify problems where solutions would be facilitated by more knowledge. Students then carry out research projects that will provide such knowledge. Other programmes, like those sponsored by ACTION (see page 151), combine voluntary work in a community service organization with a related course curriculum. One exemplary programme trains university students to train and supervise high school students as tutors of elementary school children who have reading problems. The programme has pioneered in developing techniques for training students to teach reading to children, and testing has shown a sharp rise in the reading skills of the tutored children.

Federal Programmes and LBP

The federal government has come under sharp criticism in recent years for its failure to have developed a coherent national policy on youth. Although national goals for youth development have never been officially articulated, a substantial interest in the concept of youth participation has begun to appear in the policies of many federal agencies that deal with young people. Federally-sponsored programmes that advance participation learning both reflect the policy orientation of the federal government and illustrate educational ideas that are politically acceptable. The three most prominent federal efforts to incorporate LBP principles during the 1970s have been the Experience-Based Career Education (EBCE) programmes directed by the National Institute of Education, certain programmes under the Youth Employment and Demonstration Projects Act (YEDPA) of the Department of Labor, and the service learning projects of the ACTION agency.

Career education was introduced in 1971 as a means of bringing the school curriculum into closer coordination with the world of work. By moving beyond the narrow job-training emphasis of traditional vocational education, career education aimed at giving students both a broader exposure to the range of career options available to them and a greater awareness of their own abilities and preferences. Hence, students would be better prepared to make informed career choices.

Although the basic concepts of career education have spawned a multitude of different programme approaches throughout the country, the most successful federally-sponsored programme has been Experience-Based Career Education.[9] EBCE, as it is called, is an ambitious, comprehensive programme designed to replace the regular curriculum completely. As its name states, most or all of the learning occurs during, or is related to, out-of-school experiences in a variety of community settings. Traditional, arbitrary distinctions between academic courses, vocational training, and guidance and counselling are eliminated, with all three integrated into a single, unified learning programme. Teachers' roles are redefined, with each 'learning coordinator' responsible for all phases of a student's learning (academic, vocational, personal), assisted by 'site resource persons' (cooperating adults at the community sites).

EBCE got its start in 1972, when the United States Office of Education directed each of four federally-funded regional educational laboratories[10] to design and test EBCE models with the above-mentioned features. Other mandated programme elements were:

a. primary emphasis on personal development – i.e., building students' capacity to make decisions, seek and accept responsibility, gain confidence, etc.;
b. individualization of the learning programme, with many learning options and frequent opportunities for each student to make choices about what to learn, how, when and why;
c. specific performance-based objectives, used to guide and measure student-learning in academic, career and personal development areas.

The guidelines issued to the four laboratories also stipulated that: the EBCE programme must be an educational option offered by an established 'parent' high school, and not a separate or competitive alternative school; it must be open to all students interested in learning by doing, and not a programme for dropouts; students successful in it would receive the standard diploma of the parent high school; each programme would be directed by an advisory board drawn from the community.

All four laboratories followed the same procedure for implementing and disseminating their EBCE programmes. After being created and tested in a controlled 'laboratory school' setting with 200 students representing a cross section of achievement, race and socio-economic backgrounds, each laboratory's model was then transferred to a 'demonstration site' in a local high school. The demonstration sites served to display the model to potential adopters and to provide a setting for continued programme development. The first wave of adopters were other local school systems which received free technical assistance and training, but no federal operating funds. After that, limited assistance and training was offered to other school districts that asked for EBCE in response to local needs.

EBCE thus exemplifies the strategy often employed by the federal government to advance centrally determined objectives, that is, the development of strong, transferable programme models for adoption by local practitioners. The problem with this strategy in the past has been that local factors have tended to overwhelm the preplanned programme model. It is unlikely that EBCE has escaped this fate. Of the half dozen programme sites I have visited personally, the strongest seemed to be the one in which the model had been the most changed by its local operators. This site, that is to say, had attributes of a locally-designed programme, in particular a strong, confident programme director who felt she had created her own version of EBCE according to her conception of what was most appropriate for her school and community, and what most suited the strengths of herself and her staff. At sites that were attempting to implement the model 'by the book', local EBCE personnel reported struggles to understand the rather complicated programme prescriptions. They were also concerned that some of the materials provided as part of the programme package seemed unsuited to their situation. No doubt in response to similar reports, the laboratories that first designed the programmes and have since then worked on implementing them in local school systems, have ceased to describe their implementation goal as programmes of 'high fidelity' to the model, and now stress the process of adapting programme components to individual sites.[11]

Another federal initiative with partial or potential relevance to LBP is the youth programmes administered by the Department of Labor and authorized by the Youth Employment and Development Projects Act of 1977 (YEDPA). Basically aimed at providing employment and improving the employability of out-of-work youth,

YEDPA also provided money to experiment with new approaches for helping unemployed youth. Some of these new approaches were created by local educational and community agencies, which were encouraged to design a programme and apply for funds.

YEDPA had two features that related to LBP. First, it encourages institutional links among educational, work and training systems in local communities, setting aside funds for innovative school-based programmes that ease the transition from school to work. Two priorities for these in-school demonstration projects were methods for granting academic credit for work experience and job creation through youth-operated programmes. Second, YEDPA insists on mandatory 'youth participation' in all phases of the programmes it supported. The following paragraph from a 'charter' for YEDPA issued by the Department of Labour to explain its policy gives a sample of the rhetoric being employed by the federal government:

> *Youth participation should be emphasized.* The YEDPA is based on the premise that our nation's youth are an under-utilized resource. Most young persons can fill responsible positions if they are given a chance, and responsibility is a basic element in the developmental process. Youth should, therefore, be involved at every stage of the design, implementation and administration of the new programs. The law mandates their participation in advisory councils, and the Department of Labor will establish a national youth advisory group. Public and non-profit agencies administering the programs cannot expect private employers to do what they will not. Hence, younger persons especially those who have been previous participants in career development, employment and training programs, should be hired for administrative positions whenever possible. In work experience components, here are a number of ways in which youth can serve other youth who need help. Such approaches should be emphasized.[12]

Despite the rhetorical commitment to work-related academic learning and to youth participation, YEDPA was at least neither an education programme nor a youth development programme, but rather an economic recovery act. The overwhelming emphasis was on providing money and jobs to out-of-work youth. Even the objective of encouraging young people to stay in or return to school could be seen for its economic effect of diverting some youth from the labour market, and at least temporarily from the unemployment rolls. The school-based programmes themselves were intended to focus narrowly on preparing students for work, with little attention to broader developmental goals for youth such as those of LBP. Although these essentially economic goals dominated the priorities of the local programmes created under YEDPA, some programmes nonetheless emerged that embodied LBP principles. The Department of Labor in fact asked the National Commission on Resources for Youth to help identify such programmes to serve as possible models.

After the first years of YEDPA, a number of trends could be discerned. Many of the non-school programmes were providing youth with work that made a real contribution to the community while imparting useful skills. In one programme, for example, youth removed architectural barriers to the handicapped from public buildings and installed fixtures and equipment needed by the handicapped. In another they worked with a grass-roots community development organization renovating abandoned buildings, turning vacant lots into creative playgrounds, and other such urban reclamation activities; the young people were involved in the planning and design of these projects as well as their execution. Most of these programmes stressed skills training and not other kinds of learning. Few of them established relationships with schools that would lead to credit-granting arrangements. Those programmes that did provide a systematic learning component in conjunction with the work experience tended to originate in the schools. These school-based programmes closely resembled many of the locally-originating LBP-type programmes that have been emerging over the years. Indeed, some of the already existing school-based LBP programmes were granted new life by applying for funds under YEDPA. If necessary, such programmes were modified to include the employment aspects of YEDPA: that is, pay for eligible students.

One of the YEDPA-funded programmes that clearly met LBP criteria was an ecology project in which young people met with municipal officials to chart their city's conservation needs. These planning meetings resulted in work in which youth rechannelled a stream that had been flooding, demarcated local wetlands so that roads could be built, and mapped a drainage system and catch basins. Academic credit was arranged at the high school both for the work experience and for special courses that provided the skills and knowledge for the project. In addition, a weekly seminar was conducted at the high school for discussion and reflection on the ongoing activities.

Another federal agency whose programmes may incorporate LBP is ACTION. Best known for its Peace Corps and VISTA (the 'domestic peace corps') programmes, ACTION administers a variety of programmes in poor communities. It has become an advocate of service-learning, a close relative of LBP. Service-learning programmes combine out-of-school learning for academic credit with some sort of voluntary community service for which the student usually receives some kind of compensation in the form of educational vouchers, financial assistance, or a combination of these. (Educational vouchers, or entitlements, have a monetary value that may be used to pay for future educational services. They are also being provided to youth under some of the YEDPA programmes.) Such programmes must combine a legitimate learning experience, validated by the awarding of academic credit, with a valid concept of service, which means that real community needs are being met. Several programmes sponsored by ACTION promote service-learning and LBP principles. The University Year for ACTION (UYA) programme provides grants to colleges and universities to operate volunteer programmes in which students spend a year working in community agencies in a poverty area for a small stipend. The student volunteer usually lives and works with the people in the community that the agency serves and meanwhile receives academic credit toward a degree through an experiential learning system designed by the university. The Youth Challenge Programme supports volunteer service programmes developed by high schools, colleges, or community organizations to provide service-learning opportunities for students aged 14 to 21. Student volunteers work part-time in agencies in low-income communities for a period of one year or less. The National Student Volunteer Programme is designed to provide technical assistance, training and on-site consultation to existing, locally-designed and supported student volunteer programmes. There are about 450,000 student volunteers at nearly 2,000 college campuses and 500 high schools across the United States, engaging in such activities as work with young children and the elderly, drug abuse prevention, tutoring, companionship and recreation projects, consumer education and housing improvement.

Most service learning activities for ACTION are coordinated by the National Center for Service-Learning (NCSL), which also acts as an advocate for the development and expansion of student volunteer and service learning programmes.[13] Among NCSL's support services to practitioners in the field are training workshops, on-site consultation to high school and college programmes, and the development of curriculum, planning, training, evaluation and other resource materials. NCSL also conducts research such as the national survey of high school community service programmes mentioned earlier.

In 1979—80, NCSL experimented with service-learning as a strategy for improving the education, attitudes and behaviour of young people who had been in trouble with the law. Conducted in three urban secondary schools, the Juvenile Offender Service-Learning Program involved 96 young people, aged 12 to 19, most of whom were three to five years behind academically and had a history of contacts with police and the courts. In the programme, these young people took part in service activities such as working in child-care centres, assisting the elderly, tutoring younger children and working in hospitals and clinics. To ensure the quality of their service experience, the programme insisted on certain standards:

a. for young people to consider their work worthwhile to both themselves and to the community, programmes must contribute to meeting real human or social needs;
b. young people must be responsible for their work and must have responsible work to do; young people should not be assigned routine chores and asked to peer over the shoulders of people doing the real work;
c. programmes must have measurable service and learning goals, and be well planned and managed from both the service and learning perspectives, in order that young people may extract the most learning from their work accomplishments;
d. programmes must match the community's need for assistance with the needs, skills, interest, and motivations of the young people involved.[14]

NCSL further described the programme as follows:

The Juvenile Offender Service-Learning Program is based on the general principle of individual improvement through experiential learning. By involving the youth in a combination of classroom-based academic experiences and community service activities, it is expected that positive changes will occur in his or her attitudes, behaviour, and skills. The unique approach of the program lies in the test of the service-learning experience – work performed on a voluntary basis designed to serve a social or environmental need while also providing expanded opportunities for the students to grow personally and academically – as a means of improving the youth's skills and sense of social values. Ideally, the youth participants will exhibit improvement in academic and work skills and also come to value service to others as both an intrinsically enriching experience and a stimulus to growth in self concept.

The goals of the program are the following:

(1) Students will display improvement in mathematiccs and reading skills.

(2) Students will acquire more positive attitudes about them-selves and others.

(3) Students will exhibit improvement in their adaptive work skills.

(4) Students will exhibit a reduction in the incidence of deviant behaviour.[15]

The Juvenile Offender Service Learning Program was evaluated after its first year of operation; the impact of the programme on its students was compared with changes in a control group of students from the same or other schools. Major findings of the evaluation were that:

the approach of placing troubled youths in community agencies worked well; across the different sites and student populations, the experience was, with very few exceptions, both beneficial to the student and the agencies. The volunteer work experience appeared to move the students toward some responsibility, both personally and socially, and might serve as an inducement for students to enter the world of work. For many of the students, the agency placements were their first work experience where they had duties to perform and people who were counting on them. Interestingly, nine students were offered part-time paid employment at their placements, an event which seemed to enhance the perceived value of the experience in the eyes of the students.[16]

All of the federally-supported programmes described above either were begun or thrived under the administration of President Jimmy Carter (1977-80). With the advent of the Ronald Reagan presidency in 1981, the future of many programmes that relied on federal dollars was in doubt.

LBP-Related Alternatives

LBP is less a specific programme than it is a set of principles that can be applied to many educational programmes. Several federal offices that serve specialized educational interests or populations have shown interest in LBP, and have funded efforts to identify or develop programme models adapted to their constituents. Meanwhile, LBP programmes serving these special populations or needs have been developed in local communities and schools. LBP has been successfully applied, for example, in programmes for gifted and talented youth, runaways and school dropouts, and youthful offenders. In the case of young people exhibiting deviant or antisocial behaviour, LBP is regarded hopefully as a means of prevention or diversion, which means making it available to a cross-section of the young – before deviants have been singled out for special treatement.

Many already familiar educational alternatives have similarities to LBP. Some of these, like service-learning, could be considered subforms of participation learning. Others, like career education, may or may not employ participation learning. It is indicative of the current power of the LBP idea that some older educational forms that have employed little or no participation learning in the past, such as vocational education and work-study, are now modifying their programmes to include it. Since these programmes each have their own distinct definitions and goals, it is important to distinguish them from LBP *per se*.

Vocational education.

Vocational or vocational-technical education is concerned with providing occupational skills, and is more directly concerned with giving young people advanced training and thus a head start in the occupation the student chooses. While an LBP programme may well expose young people to occupations they might choose, it also emphasizes the cultivation of more generalized personal skills and resources, such as responsibility, decision making, compassion and cooperation. In fact, an LBP programme may be seen as an opportunity for youth to be exposed to jobs in institutions they are *not* likely to choose, as a means of deepening young people's understanding of their community. LBP may also be integrated with the academic study of a related field, such as social sciences, and may readily be linked with development in the affective domain, including understanding values, group processes and personal problem solving – areas that are not usually encompassed by the vocational curriculum.

Career education.

While vocational education is a job-training design, career education aims more at choice-preparation, seeking through a variety of methods to prepare students to make informed choices about eventual employment. As such it is distinguishable from LBP in at least three dimensions. First, it is future-oriented, emphasizing preparation for future choices rather than providing opportunities to make and act on choices in the present. Second, career education is still adult-directed, that is, governed by what adult planners and futurists have charted as the most viable career fields; LBP, on the other hand, emphasizes the young people's role in structuring their present experience. Third, while career education is tied directly to potential careers, LBP, while it often involves career-related experiences, does not rule out experiences – such as the many human service or social action activities – that may bear little relation to likely future careers. Tutoring another person, for instance, or working to clean up a river have real value in the present. Furthermore, for the sake of present needs (which naturally have great relevance for the future) LBP can comprehend exposing a future laboratory technician to barn-building, or a future computer-programmer to ship's carpentry. A final difference between the two approaches is that while career education centres on the individual (for example, in the EBCE programmes, described above, individualization was totally mandatory), LBP often emphasizes group projects and working as a group toward a common goal.

Work-study.

In work-study, or cooperative education, programmes, students are given an opportunity, through an arrangement between school (usually college) and employers, to alternate or combine academic studies with paid work-experience in related fields of employment. As a form of paid job-orientation or career-exploration, it does not share LBP's central focus on opportunities for young people to engage in socially meaningful activities, often in groups, in which they exercise the responsible decision-making roles.

Youth employment programmes.

The high rate of youth joblessness has caused a whole constellation of employment and training programmes to be created. While the primary intent of these programmes is to give economic relief, they are often couched in the language of youth development. The Department of Labor, in its youth programmes (YEDPA), for example, borrowed much of the current 'transition-from-school-to-work' rhetoric, and even declares its own version of 'youth participation' mandatory. It is easy to say that any young person doing productive work is not only 'participating in society' but also probably learning something from the experience. This does not make it Learning by Participation in the sense intended here. LBP aims primarily at providing youth with maturity-producing experiences in the adult world which serve as the basis for an integrated, systematic learning-component. LBP is not a strategy for reducing youth unemployment. The factors that determine rates of youth joblessness are determined by the economic system, not by the quality of experiences enjoyed by youth in a learning programme. LBP is fundamentally an educational, not an economic, programme.

That said, however, learning by participation may nonetheless be seen as a vital strategy for improving the *employability* of youth. In an article on the relationship between participatory learning experiences and employability, Hedin asks:

> What *does* make a young person more employable? It appears that five kinds of skills and/or capacities are important. They are:
> 1. Basic academic skills, e.g., computing, reading, writing.
> 2. Complex reasoning skills, e.g., problem-solving, decision making, planning, gathering and analyzing information.
> 3. Interpersonal skills, e.g., getting along with others, willingness to take direction and accept criticism, communicating, listening and speaking skills.
> 4. Saleable skills, e.g., typing, welding, working with children;
> 5. Psychological and social maturity, e.g., positive self-regard, a sense of social and personal responsibility, self-control, self-direction, a sense of obligation to complete tasks, etc.[17]

She goes on to cite research evidence that learning by participation has been shown to enhance development in each of these categories.

Youth representation on advisory councils or policy making bodies.

While the inclusion of representatives of youth on the advisory or policy-making bodies of organizations whose activities affect young people – for example, schools and school boards, welfare commissions, recreation commissions, and hospital boards – is laudable, much needed and overdue, it is distinguishable from LBP in that the participatory experience is usually limited to the representatives alone. LBP aims at insuring active, first-hand participation for all young people, not just their representatives.

Prospects for LBP in the United States

The success of numerous diverse, individual projects has demonstrated that LBP is a viable educational alternative, but what are its prospects for truly widespread adoption?

One hopeful sign is that educational researchers have begun to take an active interest in experiential and participatory learning. Research has an important role to play in objectively validating practitioners' claims of success. At the same time, research can add systematically to our knowledge of what works best – information that is badly needed by both practitioners and policy makers. Until recently, what little research there was that related to LBP tended to be idiosyncratic and journalistic.[18] Now several research institutes are turning their attention to this field. Leading the way is the Center for Youth Development and Research at the University of Minnesota.[19] In 1982 this institute published the results of a national evaluation of experiential learning programmes, which studied the impact of four types of programmes – community service, career internships, outdoor adventure and community research – on more than 1,000 students in 27 secondary schools. Over all, the authors found that, compared to non-experiential programmes:

> experiential education programs can have a positive impact on students' psychological, social and intellectual development. Students in experiential programs tended to increase significantly, both in absolute terms and in relation to students in classroom programs, in the major scales employed in this study. These included tests of moral reasoning, self-esteem, social and personal responsibility, attitudes toward adults and others, career exploration, and empathy/complexity of thought.[20]

The authors, Conrad and Hedin, also found that, 'While the results were extremely positive on a general level, they were not invariably so. That is, on every scale there were important differences among the experiential programmes.'[21] Therefore, they sought to identify the factors within individual programmes (programme features or student characteristics) that correlated with effectiveness.

> The clearest and most significant conclusion of this study is that well-constructed experiential programs can be a powerful educational vehicle for promoting personal *and* intellectual development and can do so more effectively than classroom instruction. Programs which feature a combination of action and reflection, and which offer challenge, autonomy and collegial relationships

with adults are the ones most likely to promote student growth.[22]

Despite the growing interest in allowing greater opportunities for young people to learn through participation, formidable barriers remain, both institutional and attitudinal. Teachers worry about having to learn new methods and roles or, worse, they fear that moving students out of schools, especially at a time of declining enrolments, will mean a loss of their jobs. Students are anxious about a drastic change from familiar school life, which may mean separation from their peer culture and confrontation with a potentially hostile adult world. Parents are sceptical about having their children 'loose' in the community, and about the quality of the learning that will occur. Neither parents nor students wish to risk weakening the academic credentials that will determine their immediate future. Adults who cooperate with LBP programmes are unsure of their ability to teach or even get on well with young people. They are concerned about a programme's impact on their own work, and about legal issues, union contracts and insurance.

On a broader plane, resistance to LBP occurs when it is seen as a threat to various interests. In the economic sphere, the adult world to which young people seek access is a capitalistic one based on competitive, not helping, relations. This makes potential co-operators with LBP in the marketplace wary of any undertaking that might reduce productivity or entail additional cost. Perhaps more critical, competition for jobs dominates the labour market, and in the absence of a full-employment economy any prospective influx of new 'hands' into the world of work is likely to be looked upon with disfavour by organized labour. Furthermore, to the extent that youth participation does overlap the job market, those who will be most threatened will be the marginally employed, such as school dropouts and welfare recipients, or those disadvantaged groups, such as minorities and women, who in increasing numbers are seeking entry-level jobs.

All these factors are magnified significantly during any economic recession. Employers in both public and private sectors cut expenditures, labour suffers rising unemployment, and workers with low skills or little seniority rejoin youth in disproportionate numbers in the ranks of the jobless. The pinch is also felt by the schools, where voters demand, in the one public institution whose budget they can limit directly, an end to the 'frills' – that is, to all but the traditional core programme.

Minority groups rightly detect in out-of-school learning schemes an implicit danger that it will become a new way of tracking the educationally disadvantaged. In many American high schools, 'alternative programme' has already become the recognized euphemism for a special programme that segregates academically or socially 'maladjusted' students. It is not difficult to imagine how schools might distort LBP as a device for ridding their premises of such 'difficult' students.

On the other hand, the schools themselves are a potential source of resistance to LBP reforms. American schools historically have promoted conformity and control as social goods that were central to their role. Dedicated to mass education and managerial efficiency, they have never been receptive to any substantial degree either to special programme alternatives, which smacked of elitism, or to basic reforms that served the developmental needs of children before the bureaucratic needs of the institution. All these strains in traditional American schooling collide with the aims of LBP, which promotes responsibility and initiative for youth, and seeks institutional reform that meets the positive developmental needs of adolescents.

Overarching these institution- and interest-based barriers to LBP are societally-held attitudes that may be the most difficult of all to overcome. Americans tend to be ungenerous in their views toward youth. Like other powerless minorities, young people are often condemned for having 'chosen' group traits that merely reflect a societally imposed predicament. Such an approach has become known as a 'blame the victim' explanation for societal failure. Denied the experiences they need to reach maturity, youth nevertheless are accused of immaturity, which in turn is used to show they are not 'ready' to participate in society. Similarly, adults distrust youth because youth has values and a lifestyle that seems to reject those of adults; they fail to consider how their own rejection of youth has made an enclosed, opposing youth culture inevitable.

Over the past twenty years, Americans have spent vast sums of money in various attempts to bring about social and educational change. The failure of most of these efforts to produce the desired changes has added up to a very expensive lesson in the kinds of government intervention that are likely to be effective. A key finding from attempts to change school practice has been that local practitioners are powerful enough to block innovations of which they do not approve, and that a condition they impose on that approval is participation in the planning and implementation of the change itself. In accordance with this finding, the federal government has modified its traditional change strategy of funding the development of 'proven', transferable, programme models on the assumption that they would be passively adopted by local practitioners. Government change-efforts now aim more at encouraging local invention by offering material support for programme ideas that stem from the grass roots. The Department of Labor made money available to local programmes using this approach, and a number of existing LBP programmes whose futures were in doubt found new life under YEDPA.

The new approach augurs well for the kinds of locally-originating youth participation programmes that have been so effective individually. It means that future programme designs will be diverse, reflecting local perceptions of local conditions – needs, people and resources. There are no standard solutions to the problems posed by the planning of a new LBP programme, problems such as scheduling, transportation, criteria for credit, staffing, community supervision, costs. Solutions to these problems should be the product of local problem-solving, not only because there is no better way to assure that the solutions fit local circumstances, but also because the problem-solving process is an important device for building programme strength and commitment. This is not to say, of course, that local planners cannot learn from solutions devised elsewhere. The experience of others is a valuable teacher, particularly because it has a real-world validity that speaks directly to other practitioners. But these experiences should be seen as a source of inspiration, not imitation.

LBP aims to reintegrate youth into a society that itself has become fragmented. To meet the requirements of a complex, technologically advanced world, organizations and institutions have taken on separate and highly specialized roles, representing distinct, often competing interests. The organizational specialization of schools, business, unions, and government has limited the means by which society may achieve its broader goals such as the rounded development of its youth. These transcendent goals require cooperative interrelationships among schools and segments of society that have been content to leave education exclusively to the schools. LBP is thus more than an institutional reform affecting schools alone; it is also a societal reform that requires the participation and collaboration of social institutions heretofore uninvolved.

There are also some more pragmatic reasons why these different community sectors must be actively involved. Government policies affecting local communities have long recognized the necessity of establishing local representative councils made up of those groups whose cooperation is necessary for programmes to be effective. EBCE, for example, requires that each programme site establish a community advisory council that includes local representatives of business, unions, industry, government, education, parents and students, and that has both policy-making and advisory responsibilities. Through long, hard experience, reformers have come to understand that change in social and bureaucratic institutions (many, like schools, are both) takes place as the result of a gradual process that is highly political in nature. Local interest groups are strong enough to block any programmes they do not support. In return for their cooperation they demand participation in the planning and decision making that determines the shape of the programme, in other words, in the change process itself. Their participation in this process appears to be the only way to assure the sense of commitment and ownership that is necessary for a programme to be successfully implemented and to continue to be supported politically. Thus reformers today speak of planned change as a matter of initiating a process rather than designing and selling a programme. With the critical power of participation thus gaining increasing recognition from policy planners, one might expect the logic of participation for youth to grow more and more compelling. That logic seems one of the last principles determining social change only means that winning acceptance of LBP will continue to be a struggle against odds.

Notes and References

1. COLEMAN, J.S. *et al.*, (1966). *Equality of Educational Opportunity*. Washington, D.C.: United States Government Printing Office; JENCKS, C. *et al.*, *Inequality: A Reassessment of the Effect of Family and Schooling in America*. New York: Basic Books, 1972.
2. HAVIGHURST, R.J., GRAHAM, R. and EBERLY, D. (1972). 'American Youth in the Mid-Seventies, *Bulletin of the National*

Association of Secondary School Principals. No. 56, November, 1972; National Commission on the Reform of Secondary Education (BROWN, B.F. Chair) (1973). *The Reform of Secondary Education.* New York: McGraw-Hill. COLEMAN, JAMES S. (1972). (Chair), *Youth: Transition to Adulthood.* Report of the President's Science Advisory Committee. Chicago: University of Chicago Press. GIBBONS, M. (1976). *The New Secondary Education: A Phi Delta Kappa Task Force Report.* Bloomington, Indiana: Phi Delta Kappa. National Commission on Manpower Policy, *From School to Work: Improving the Transition.* Washinton, D.C.: U.S. Government Printing Office, No. 040-000-00364-9, 1976; National Panel on High School and Adolescent Education, *The Education of Adolescents: The Final Report and Recommendations.* Washington, D.C.: U.S. Government Printing Office, No. (OE) 76-00004, 1976; TYLER, R.W. (ed) (1978). *From Youth to Constructive Adult Life: The Role of the Public School.* Berkeley, California: McCutchan. Carnegie Council of Policy Studies in Higher Education, *Giving Youth a Better Chance: Options for Education, Work and Service.* San Francisco, California: Jossey-Bass, 1979; National Commission on Youth, *The Transition of Youth to Adulthood: A Bridge Too Long.* Boulder, Colorado: Westview Press, 1980.

3. NATIONAL COMMISSION ON RESOURCES FOR YOUTH (1974). *New Roles for Youth in the School and the Community.* New York: Citation Press. McCLOSKEY, MILDREN and KLEIN-BARD, PETER (1974). *Youth Into Adult: Nine Selected Youth Participation Programs.* New York: The National Commission on Resources for Youth.

4. NATIONAL CENTER FOR SERVICE-LEARNING (1979). 'National Survey: High School Student Community Service Programs'. Washington, D.C.: National Center for Service-Learning, 1979.

5. BERMAN, P. and McLAUGHLIN, M.W. (1975). *Federal Programs Supporting Educational Change, Vol. IV: The Findings in Review.* Santa Monica, California: The Rand Corp.

6. WIGGINTON, E. (ed.), (1972-82). *The Foxfire Books, 1-7.* Garden City, NY: Anchor Books.

7. DOLLAR, B. (1975). *Youth Participation: A Concept Paper.* New York: National Commission on Resources for Youth.

8. Information on programmes in all categories can be obtained from the National Commission on Resources for Youth, Inc., 36 West 44th Street, New York, New York 10036.

9. Special issue (1976) *Illinois Career Education Journal: Experience-Based Career Education.* 33:3, Spring.

10. The four were Appalachia Educational Laboratory (Charlestown, West Virginia); Far West Laboratory (San Francisco, California); Northwest Regional Educational Laboratory (Portland, Oregon); and Research for Better Schools (Philadelphia, Pennsylvania).

11. EBCE has been extensively evaluated. Information on this research is

available from: Far West Laboratories for Educational Research and Development, 1855 Folsom Street, San Francisco, California 94103; and Northwest Regional Educational Laboratory, 710 S.W. Second Avenue, Portland, Oregon 97204.

12.   *A Planning Charter for the Youth Employment and Demonstration Projects Act of 1977*, Washington, D.C.: US Department of Labor, Employment and Training Administration, Office of Youth Programs, August, pp. 5-6.

13.   More information on service-learning may be obtained from the National Center for Service-Learning, 806 Connecticut Avenue N.W. Room 1106, Washington D.C. 20525.

14.   NATIONAL CENTER FOR SERVICE LEARNING, (1981). *Evaluation of Juvenile Offender Service-Learning Study*. Washington, D.C.: ACTION, Office of Policy and Planning, p. 5.

15.   ibid., pp. 1-2.

16.   ibid., pp. 2-3.

17.   HEDIN, D. (1980). 'Youth Participation in Youth Employment Programs,' in *Post-Conference Proceedings, National Youth Participation Conference*. Washington, D.C.: U.S. Department of Labor, Office of Youth Programs, p. 118.

18.   A notable exception is in the area of tutoring by youth, a major form of learning by participation. Cross-age and peer tutoring have been quite thoroughly studied, and shown to be effective in producing sometimes dramatic gains in learning and other dimensions of growth, especially for tutors. Two books that both review the research on tutoring by youth and contain excellent bibliographies are: ALLEN, V.L. (ed) (1979) *Children as Teachers*. New York: Academic Press, 1976; and Sinclair Goodlad, *Learning by Teaching*. London: Community Service Volunteers.

19.   The Center for Youth Development and Research, University of Minnesota, 1985 Buford Avenue, St. Paul, Minnesota 55108.

20.   CONRAD, D. and HEDIN, D. (1982). *Executive Summary of the Final Report of the Experiential Education Evaluation Project*. St. Paul, Minnesota: Center for Youth Development and Research, University of Minnesota, p. 35.

21.   ibid., p. 35.

22.   ibid., p. 43.

CHAPTER FIVE
Scandinavia

MAGNE SKRINDO

The governments of the Scandinavian countries have been Europe's most active in instituting social welfare reforms, many centring on educational systems. Ironically, these very reforms have led to conditions which at the same time make LBP more necessary AND impede it; the hierarchical administrative control considered necessary to implement them and the emphasis on equality of opportunity in education has led to a degree of standardization and uniformity such that innovations such as LBP have great difficulty taking hold unless they are adopted as national policy. Nevertheless, a grass-roots movement has begun to stir in Scandinavia in the form of locally-initiated programmes. Magne Skrindo describes the conditions in Norway, Denmark and Sweden that have given rise to these efforts, and invokes the need for LBP to be reflected in national priorities. Mr. Skrindo is a lecturer at Sagene College of Education in Oslo, and is editor of a professional journal in Norway.

Introduction

Recently a middle school in Norway undertook three projects: the restoration of an old boat, a farm blacksmith's shop and a mill. The boat, which had begun to rot and decompose, is now used by the pupils of the school to take sailing trips on the fjord. The blacksmith's shop was one of the last in existence in the area and was also in the process of decaying. The farmer partially restored the mill, but the pupils completed the work and also reconstructed the 400-metre-long channel which brought water to the mill. Finally the young people ground some grain, took the flour to the school and made some 'old' food for the end-of-term celebration. Now the pupils are able to study and engage in the handwork and technology

165

which was common in farming and the fishing industry in their region for hundreds of years.[1]

What do these activities have to do with schooling?

Ten years ago the answer to this question would in all probability have been 'Nothing'. It certainly was not for such activities that, during the 1950s, policy-makers and educationalists laid plans for the nine-year, compulsory Scandinavian unified or comprehensive schools. The main intention was to give all children and young people, regardless of social or ethnic background, sex or geographic derivation, an equal opportunity for schooling. That aim, by and large, has been realized; access to education is probably more readily available for the children of unskilled workers, farmers or fishermen in Scandinavia than in any country in Europe. But at the same time, the activities at the school in the west of Norway, which we mentioned, give an account of the Scandinavian school in crisis.

The Scandinavians have used enormous resources to construct a system which conforms to conventional modern concepts of school, education, teaching, instruction and learning. Today, the Scandinavians must recognize that they have achieved what they planned for, but that it has not turned out to be all they had hoped for. In short, we see that large numbers of pupils in the nine-year comprehensive as well as in the three-year secondary (ages 16 to 19) schools do not always receive significant education. At all levels in the system (classroom, school, local community, county, state, research bodies) people are making great efforts to deal with or solve the problems.

Up to now, in Denmark, Norway and Sweden, there has been no specific project which can be called Learning by Participation. But the LBP concepts and principles which were outlined in Chapter One are often used in educational debates and are the basis of a number of research activities. Activity-oriented educationalists such as John Dewey (1859—1952), George Kerschensteiner (1854—1932) and William H. Kilpatrick (1871—1965) have had considerable influence on educational thought and course planning, and occasionally also on educational practice. In this chapter, we will describe and discuss some examples which roughly parallel the LBP movement in other countries. Our intention is to contribute to comparative analysis and discussions on the present 'educational crisis'.

Tradition and systems

We have selected and analysed LBP examples which stress those features of the Scandinavian tradition which are inspired by the ideal of freedom. Questions central to this tradition hinge on *the pupil's own influence on the choice of activities, experiences and learning situations offered.* Furthermore, we will make some evaluation, based on learning theory, as to *genuine pupil activity.* Finally, we shall take a position with regard to the discrepancy between our ideals and principles, and the reality experienced by many Scandinavian pupils and teachers.

The principle of equal and fair opportunity for all has long been central to the development of educational systems in Scandinavia. The comprehensive or one-school-for-all principle has been achieved in the compulsory basic school (ages 7 to 16) and is now being implemented for the secondary schools (ages 16 to 19).

Further, stress is being placed on the integration of functions and developments in the ordinary schools which might be considered barriers to the above principles; and opportunities are given to adults to receive the education they may have been deprived of, unjustly, in their youth. (In Norway about 99 per cent of all children between the ages of seven and 16 are integrated in the ground school.)

Denmark, Norway and Sweden established compulsory education relatively early in Europe. The beginnings of such regulations can be seen as early as 1750—1850, when the Lutheran State Church maintained that such education should be instituted. After this, mass primary schools were challenged to take on this responsibility as political democracy took shape, mainly as a consequence of the peasant movement in the 1800s and the workers' movement in the 1900s. Public acceptance of compulsory schooling has long been relatively higher than in other European countries.

The planning and development of the present school system started around 1950. At that time there was a marked development in industrialization, mechanization and centralization of production and population. Unemployment and poverty were rapidly becoming mere memories of the 1930s. The social democratic parties, which were in power in all three countries, had strong support from the electorate in the development of state economic planning, the welfare state, and increased educational opportunities for all. Educational expansion was considered a necessary condition of continuing economic growth and universally improved living standards.

In the 1950s and 1960s considerable increases in expenditure were possible. New schools and school buildings were built, the production of teaching aids increased considerably, and the number of teachers and administrators rose sharply. A steadily increasing number of children and young people were given the opportunity to spend more time at school, especially in rural districts. To mention but a few examples, working days at rural folk schools were extended from three to five days a week; the school-leaving age was raised to include nine not seven years of schooling, and the secondary schools (*gymnas*) were established in practically all districts.

The expansion of schools and educational programmes has been extensive during the past thirty years. Organizational and administrative systems have also been developed as a part of the general expansion. Many new administrative positions have been created and a considerable educational bureaucracy has grown up.

All policy, legal and economic decisions in Scandinavia are made by politically-elected bodies. During the actual process of decision-making, any individual is free to exert influence; this applies both to ordinary citizens and those directly affected by decisions. For example, educational decisions are influenced greatly by direct participation of teachers, parents and administrators. However, when a decision finally has been made, such as in Parliament, its application is a purely administrative matter. In practice, there is little difference between the educational organization and those concerned with social welfare, health, communication, etc. The administrative system is hierarchical, with decision-making authority 'at the top', and delegated authority at the lower levels.

Within the hierarchal educational organizations reforms are carried out more or less as follows: first, the government appoints a committee, which works over a long period of time – up to several years – conducting hearings, producing detailed reports and making recommendations. This material is published, so that any member of the public can have access to it, take part in discussions on it, and express opinions. Statements of opinion from teachers' organizations, parent groups, professional unions (the National Trade Union, the National Employers' Union, etc.), political organs in communities and counties, political parties and so on, will be of special interest in this connection. All statements are evaluated by the Department of Education and may thus influence decision-making on legislation, teaching plans, teaching aids, granting of funds and so on. When the final legislation has been passed, the process of carrying it out begins. The Department works out guidelines and instructions, circulates information and gives courses for key figures in the administration, aiming at the implementation of the reforms on a national scale within a few years.

Factors inhibiting LBP

The educational systems of Scandinavia can point to many encouraging results in their reform efforts. In an international context, the situation can probably be described as exemplary. The following points may be mentioned:

1. Large groups of children and young people have been given new and fairer opportunities; inequality, discrimination and school 'losers' still exist, but the schools offer possibilities (which could be improved!) of overcoming these difficulties.
    2. Schools for children (aged seven to 13) and young people (aged 14 to 18) have become meeting grounds for individuals with widely varying social backgrounds and value perspectives, which, at the minimum, ensure some contact and mutual understanding between social and racial groups.
    3. A system has been developed which combines state, county, and community participation, and which ensures all schools in the country of comparable and stable financial support.

Although this can be considered as natural progress within a political democracy, it is still important. But political educationalists, teachers and administrators cannot be complacent. In looking at current school problems, they must admit that expansion has been mainly in terms of outer framework and quantitative factors ('everyone has got more of traditional schooling'), and schooling has achieved the basic principles and qualitative factors of learning and socialization only minimally. Precisely because of this, the LBP movement is interesting in any discussion of the educational situation in Scandinavia.

A central feature of LBP is a demand that the school must have a clear understanding of learning and socialization as well as the usual answers to didactic and methodological questions. The beginning of the learning situation for LBP is that the pupil exercise independent and responsible choice, participate in necessary community activities, and integrate practical and critical reflection. Concretely, one begins by dealing with the pupil as an individual, and as a member of an independent pupil group, as well as with teachers as managers.

In Scandinavia this means that the LBP movement runs into difficulties with some of the other consequences of the democratic educational expansion. A political democracy must provide equal and fair opportunities for all. In concrete terms, this requires certain forms of *standardization*. In schools standardization is not only a question of time, class size, practical and economic factors. It applies, also, to the content and organization of the learning situation: syllabus, teaching aids, methods, evaluation/examinations, teacher qualifications, etc. If a class in the middle school (ages 14 to 16) decides to restore an old boat, one discovers immediately that the school's teaching approach and staff qualifications become irrelevant. Further, the pupils may work so far outside the syllabus that they may risk problems in examinations designed to compare them with other pupils. Pupils may experience significant learning and socialization in an LBP project, only to be penalized because they have not read particular books.

So the hierarchical administrative control, with its standardization of learning situations and content, represents a serious obstacle to LBP principles in Scandinavia. In the following pages, we consider two factors: the schools' content (curricula) and their evaluation system.

Within each country, a considerable *uniformity of content* is stressed. Subject aims are uniform, and in central subjects, such as native language, mathematics and foreign languages, much emphasis is placed on giving each child the best possible instruction, through teaching plans, textbooks and teaching aids. Consequently, centrally-designed material takes on more importance in such a context than local material, heavily populated centres become more important than outlying districts, urban culture is emphasized more than rural culture, even in villages, and – most important of all – theoretical or verbalized knowledge is given more significance than practical knowledge.

Such standards for the uniformity of content do not coincide very well with LBP principles. But if schools could indeed link themselves to necessary work and other activities in the community, organize periods for critical reflection about their practice, and relate these to study about other milieus and communities, it is probable that a common national fund of knowledge would be developed. It is, therefore, not only the demand for a common curriculum, but also for an evaluation system which is linked to it, which presents difficulties for LBP principles.

The evaluation system in Scandinavia is intended, simultaneously, to satisfy two goals: in part, pupils demonstrate what they know and what their motivations are for further study; in part, pupils are sorted into groups which are given different rights/opportunities in the future. In his or her class, a teacher can give marks to satisfy the first goal, but final, normed, tests and written examinations satisfy the other goal, or sorting function. The most important thing is not to find out what pupils know in relationship to a subject of study or work area, but what they know in relationship to each other. For pupils, it becomes more important to compete with each other than to illuminate their real competence in a subject. Both for pupils and teachers the central concern becomes one of working diligently with the centrally-determined subject matter; otherwise, the whole class might receive bad marks. LBP principles are not threatening to this system as long as they pertain only to optional courses, which are not graded. (The time used to restore the boat, blacksmith's shop and mill, mentioned before, was taken from optional courses.)

LBP principles in practice

In this section we shall describe and assess some projects which appear to conform, more or less, to the LBP movement in other countries. It is possible to select interesting examples from kindergarten through to higher education, but our focus in this volume is on adolescents, although we do emphasize that LBP principles are as valid for the education of young children as for that of mature adults.[2]

In Scandinavia, the schools which conform to the typical understanding of secondary education are the last three grades of the basic school (grades 7, 8 and 9) and the secondary school or *gymnas* (ages 14 to 18 or 19). Our choice of examples covers three conditions:

1. the situation of *young people with schooling problems*, because this also indicates much about the schools' shortcomings;
2. attempts to *integrate the school and the community*, because pupils necessarily move into the community if they are to engage in important and meaningful activities;
3. attempts generally to *improve teaching and instruction*, because LBP principles, if they are to have any future, must also function within that perspective.

Discussion of these examples will attempt to take into account (1) *the pupils' influence and activity*, (2) their *participation in the social environment*, (3) to what extent this participation generates *relevant criticism and theory*, (4) changes in *pupil and teacher roles* and (5) *results achieved*. However, the discussion is not always complete, since the examples come from various sources.[3]

Adolescents with schooling problems

A number of adolescents experience serious problems. At school they have difficulty in meeting the demands made on them in basic subjects; they get poor marks (grades); lose motivation for school work, feel inferior to other pupils, seek attention through anti-social behaviour, perhaps begin to play truant, seek a stronger identity through narcotics, and so on. Sometimes their self-confidence seems to be so severely weakened that they have difficulty in deciding on a vocation or a choice of further education, and thus often remain unemployed, even in areas where the rate of unemployment is low.

There are, of course, many reasons for the existence of these problems, and they are not all to be found in the schools. But the use of a generally distributed set of marks (grades) in the compulsory secondary school is a frequent cause of problems. Another important factor is the priority given to verbal and theoretical knowledge.[4, 5]

There are a number of examples of the rehabilitating effect of socially meaningful work, such as work in an agricultural collective, or work to rehabilitate young people in crisis situations. The following discussion will consider more school-orientated examples.

Vocational work as an educational option (Norway)

There has been disagreement in the Scandinavian countries about the increase in length of compulsory education from seven to nine years and about the organization of the seventh to ninth years. When the nine-year school was introduced in Norway, the eighth and ninth years were at first divided into secondary school and vocational school preparatory courses; then later into three streams which concentrate on the basic subjects of Norwegian, Maths and English, and finally, after 1974, into mixed-ability classes, with the emphasis on individualization.

The nine-year school has, ever since its introduction around 1960, had difficulties with a number of ninth-year and, to some extent, eighth-year pupils. Even with optional subjects, school was too theoretical for these young people, and the evaluation system increased their feelings of failure. A law amendment of 1975 gave more freedom of choice, including the option of spending part of the school week *at a place of work outside school.*

Many local councils have tried to find emergency solutions for truancy problems, one of which has been beginner-jobs in industry, sometimes combined with part-time schooling. However, a small number of pupils have still failed to complete the nine-year school.

The National Council for Innovation in Education began a project[6] in 1974 which replaced some of the earlier emergency measures adopted by local councils. Its aims have been to expand the accepted definition of *allmenndanning* (general education) to include vocational as well as theoretical subjects, to give schools and local councils a larger say in course content and administration, and to achieve a more flexible relationship between the school's demands and the pupil's potential.

Work on the project has developed in two main directions:

1. an increase in options throughout the nine-year school and especially in the eighth and ninth years;
2. an option, combining one or two days a week in a beginner's job, with three or four days at school concentrating on basic subjects (Norwegian, Maths, English and religious instruction).

A third alternative, in some places, has been participation in local cultural and spare-time activities.

Results.

There have been encouraging results for all alternative programmes. Reports confirm that participating pupils show more interest in school work, including the compulsory basic subjects.

Problems.

The greatest problems are found among the group which chooses to work outside school for one or two days a week in their ninth year. There has been a clear tendency for the pupils with the lowest achievement in basic subjects to choose this alternative; and it is very difficult for the school to provide a real learning situation in the pupils' working day. What they actually learn depends, to a large extent, on the goodwill of the other workers – though this is often considerable.

There has been no attempt to use enthusiastic workmates as 'teachers', but the school and the firms involved each appoint a 'contact' person. Study brochures on the various jobs in shops, industry, agriculture, forestry, building, printing – are being put together on a local basis.[7]

In many areas, the combination of work and school is interpreted as an 'inferior' choice for 'losers'. This interpretation is reinforced by the difficulty many participants in the programme find in getting a place in a high school in those areas where places are still competed for. *Thus, learning in an outside job is still not considered equal to learning in a school situation.* The inferior status of vocational work in the ninth year and in many areas is underlined by the fact that pupils choosing this alternative come predominantly from working-class backgrounds.

The project was completed in 1979. Now the decision has been taken that, by their own choice, pupils in all forms of the nine-year school can spend some hours on out-of-school activities. In a statement the Minister of Education suggested that younger pupils could pay visits to help entertain elder people (singing, reading to them and so on) while pupils in the upper forms could participate in the social services or go to an ordinary place of work. He emphasized that it was very important for teachers to link lessons in main subjects to pupils' experience in out-of-school activities.

Abak Efterskole (Denmark).

This is a continuation school, just outside the fishing community of Abenra, on the South-East coast of Jutland, and is one of a number of private boarding schools in Denmark which are designed to provide an alternative to the usual programmes found in the regular school in grades eight, nine, and ten. (Continuation schools in Denmark are provided for students from 14 to 18 years of age, on the same 'free' basis as folk high schools (folkenhøgskolder).)

The school was started in 1970 and contains approximately 55 pupils at any given time. It has struggled to evolve a functional combination of practical work with theoretical education in order to give its pupils a more honest sense of work in social life. The school has opened its doors to the extent that it blends with the major occupational activities of the community, especially with fishing, farming, carpentry and mechanical work.

The pupils have learnt little at their previous schools and many of them come to the school as drop-outs. The school staff make frequent use of practical work and practical situations as a springboard for reflection, discussion and theoretical teaching. This is partly because practical work gives the pupils new and meaningful opportunities, and partly because the practical situations give rise to a need for reflection and discussion.

After 10 years the school still has far more applicants than it has places. Pupils who have completed the course have proved to be capable of finding and keeping work.[8]

Veslestua, Skedsmo (outside Oslo, Norway).

This 'school' began in 1977 as an emergency arrangement for drop-outs from the eighth and, particularly, the ninth forms, and started with about ten pupils in an old private house. In May, 1978, its head commented: 'It does not take long to discover that the overwhelming priority in this job is to help our pupils regain confidence in themselves and their abilities. It was shattering to see how few of them had any self-respect left at all.'

Days during the first part of the 1977—8 school year followed the following pattern: the morning would begin with a meeting at which pupils and teachers would plan the day's work and read the local paper. The next two to three hours were spent on work in basic subjects (Norwegian, Maths, English). One of these hours was used for what was known as 'theoretical practice', i.e. developing the pupils' insight into the practical activities they were engaged in at other times during the week. The afternoon was spent working on their own school buildings; for example, turning one building into an arts and crafts workshop. The pupils worked in groups according to personal preference. Two days a week were spent on vocational practice, including hairdressing, carpentry and work in a bookshop. The teachers followed progress here too.

In the second half of the first school year the buildings were completed, and work was started on social and science projects. In the spring much time was spent working on the outside of the building. After the first year all the ninth-class pupils wanted to go on to secondary schools.

The second year was also a success for the school. One of the pupils appeared in a TV programme on school problems and a book was written about the school.[9] According to the teachers, it is not difficult to find suitable work-assignments for the pupils. Typical ones have been the building of an extension to the school and chopping wood in the forests for old people in the village. The wood-chopping made enough profit to finance a stay at a camp school in England at the end of the second school year.

The teachers' experience shows that pupils are more interested in practical work at the beginning of the year, but later express a need for more theory and also for ordinary school subjects, partly because they often decide that they want to take their secondary school examinations after all.

The pupils are able to exert a strong influence on the form and content of their daily activities, partly through the school council meetings attended by all pupils and teachers.[10]

Discussion.

In looking at vocational work as a school option, we consider problems as they are seen from the top of the hierarchy, with examples of the kinds of measures which are possible from that position: legislation, new plans, information, encouraging official statements, granting of funds, etc. In the description of Åbak

Efterskole and Veslestua we consider teachers' and pupils' experience in concrete learning situations.

In the examples given above, great importance was placed on giving pupils the opportunity to make choices and influence their own learning situations. At Åbak, important factors to consider are the pupils' voluntary applications for places at the school, and the opportunity for independent activity provided by the practical nature of the situation. At Veslestua, the school council attended by all pupils and teachers is an important organ for decision-making. Pupils choosing vocational work as an option at school have certainly made their own choice; however it has to be noted that the advice given by the school may make this freedom of choice delusory.

The pupils in these three examples have previously experienced defeat in most of their work in theoretical school subjects. Now they experience practical knowledge, with the possibility of acting upon their surroundings and even experiencing their action as having immediate meaning, rather than being meaningful only in some obscure future context. In this way pupils are given opportunities and challenges in fields which may be new to them, and in which they have certainly not experienced failure.

The practical work assignments are, perhaps, especially significant because the pupils experience their own activity as important to themselves and to other people or in a larger production context. Both this social recognition and the successful experience of learning how to do a concrete work task are important factors in the building up of self-confidence and a feeling of identity.

Åbak Efterskole and Veslestua seem to have succeeded in connecting work and critical reflection on the work done, and in connecting school activity to wider and more theoretical forms of learning.

The teacher's contribution to this process seems to be important. At Veslestua it is interesting to note that a new 'subject' called *theoretical practice* has been introduced; it is probably in just this field that Åbak and Veslestua have their greatest strength.

In vocational work as a school option, the question of whether pupils take part in critical reflection on their vocational practice, or whether their experience of practice is later related to school subject, remains open. No one at any of the work places has, so far, had responsibility for the pupils' learning experience, and the pupils' school teachers do not follow up the pupils' experience in a way which can lead to real critical discussion. This seems to be a major weakness of the projects.

The description of pupil and teacher roles is somewhat incomplete. But the examples show pupils experiencing forms of activity, co-operation, independence and responsibility which may well be completely absent in ordinary school programmes. The teacher's role at Åbak and Veslestua seems to have shifted away from ordinary teaching towards planning, facilitating and participating in the pupils' learning processes. The teachers talk *to* the pupils, not *at* them, and they help them to talk to each other. In the 'Vocational Work as an Option' project, the teacher's role and responsibility seems undefined.

Common to these examples is the pupils' opportunity to make choices, exert influence, and experience learning- and work-assignments which are practically and socially meaningful. Even if much remains undone in the field of teacher follow-up, in terms of critical discussion and theory, the principles involved do seem clearly to be effective in helping young people who have a history of serious difficulties at school.

School and the local environment

Teaching in the Norwegian nine-year compulsory school, in all 400 to 500 communes, follows the general guidelines laid down by the Department of Education in the *Mønsterplan for grunnskolen*. The plan requires all school subjects to be taught according to national educational aims stated by law; but it does no more than indicate a general frame of reference for teaching. Its description of topics, themes, methods and learning activities is intended to provide suggestions only, and may be adapted or added to. Local environment studies is an example of a subject which lends itself to such adaptations or additions. However, any changes which might be considered are, in fact, greatly limited by the requirement that textbooks be approved by the Department of Education, and by the fact that teaching material is normally produced only for sale in all schools. In the basic subjects (Norwegian, Mathematics and English) change is limited further by the use of standardized tests and national examination systems.

Local environment studies within such a centralized system often means 'extra work' for the teacher, who may, perhaps, have moved to the area only recently and thus may know little about it. For these reasons, education authorities, in the commune or county, encourage the production of study units, films, tapes, etc., on local topics. In many cases the work is linked with biology, social science or Norwegian lessons.

Finnmark County.

This is the northernmost Norwegian county, bordering on the Soviet Union and Finland, having 20 communes, a population of 75,000, a large Lappish group and a small Finnish immigrant group. Finnmark has developed local study-units in all its communes. The project was launched in 1973 by the county director of education. Some of the principles behind the project were stated as follows:

The project aims at breaking with the traditional Norwegian concept of general education which is enforced in Norwegian schools as though it were a 'law of nature'. The aim is, rather, an education more adapted to local and regional conditions.

The Norwegian school's present-day aims, content, organization and form are based on premises which originated in urban, densely populated areas. The resulting school units were quite unsuitable for use in outlying districts with small, scattered populations.

Textbooks and teaching materials have also been orientated towards the central areas of population and influence, while hardly mentioning Finnmark and Northern Norway.

Entrance requirements for teacher training have discriminated against young people from Northern Norway, because the area has a smaller number of secondary schools. Teachers pass on to their pupils the textbook culture they grew up with; they may know a great deal about the Brømsebro treaty in the 17th century, but they are unlikely to know anything at all about line-fishing or filleting.

Assuming that most children will remain in the area where they grow up, school must give them an education which makes them better equipped to live productively in the area. A forward-looking school will be more contemporary in its outlook and, therefore, more controversial. Schools will begin to play a positive part in the conservation and development of local districts. They must be more political than at present, without letting party politics dominate. Teachers must dare, for the sake of the coming generation, to bring the discussion of important local issues into the schools, in order to help young people become aware of the society they live in and of how they themselves want it to develop. Teachers must remember that many young people will occupy, within ten years after leaving school, important positions in society and have a say in its development.

Results.

According to the Director of Education in Finnmark the project mentioned above has contributed to an improvement of school/ community relations. When schools are teaching about local affairs and producing newspapers or magazines, local people became more interested in school affairs too. (Local newspapers and local radio started to present material from the project.)

Projects have developed in directions undreamed of in 1973. Examples of developments include work with local history collections, the establishment of camp schools, and direct contributions to the establishment of a protected (rehabilitation) industry.

According to many reports, the project has been a great success with the pupils involved. Normally, passive pupils show a new enthusiasm in local project work. This is probably because the work increases their perception of the relationship between school and the world outside.[11]

Lofoten.

In Lofoten (which has 4 communes, a population of 30,000, and is famous for one of the world's oldest cod fisheries) work began in 1973 on a project for local environment work in middle schools. The project has been coordinated by the new University of Northern Norway in Tromsø.

The project leader points out that work connected with the local community is desirable in educational terms in all schools. It is especially critical in small, outlying communities, where depopulation is a serious problem, and where neglect of it will contribute to a complete breakdown of these communities. In many outlying districts a socially relevant school is therefore imperative.

The project leader has particularly encouraged teamwork among teachers as well as cooperation between the school and the local community. Study units ('Lofoten yesterday, today and tomorrow'), tapes, and film strips have been produced. In his analysis the project leader lists the difficulties involved: the pressure of the centrally devised school syllabus and timetable, strained budgets, lack of qualified teachers, and pupils' inability to work independently.

Work on the Lofen project has followed two working methods:

a. Material about the local community is taught traditionally; that is, local issues are 'translated' into school 'subjects';
b. New rules are evolved as to relevant learning and activity in schools. This method has been used with considerable success in the so-called 'Lofot week', when school has been 'stopped' and time is devoted to local studies. The projects of this week include involvement in cod fishing, old buildings, animal and bird life, the local church, old pictures, a small outlying fishing village, a picture map of Lofoten, a theatre drop with a Lofoten scene, a model of a fisherman's hut, and rope-making.

In 1978 and 1979 the University had no more money for continued work on the project. Work on projects at several local schools stopped, but at a limited number of schools, good progress is still being made, mainly because these schools have retained teachers who are familiar with local conditions and aware of their importance in the pupils' development. These teachers have also established an efficient project administration outside the formal school administration.

Tromsø University is at the present moment engaged on a survey of the effects of a number of locally-orientated projects.[12]

The Pioneer School (Nybyggerskolen).

In Gildeskål, Northern Norway, there is a fjord village which is experiencing a high rate of depopulation. The villagers formerly made a living by combining agriculture, fishing, and hunting. As part of an effort to revitalize the village, a school was started in the autumn of 1978, its intention being to teach young people the knowledge and skills necessary to take up the old ways of making a living. A building which used to be used as a primary school was selected and in the first year 12 students were admitted. These were divided into three groups of four, and group activities rotated every third week. The main fields of activity were:

1. household skills such as baking bread, the preparation of slaughtered animals, and conducting other domestic tasks;
2. fishing with small boats, nets and equipment;
3. agriculture: growing potatoes, care of sheep, hens, rabbits and pigs, ditching, garden work and so on.

All the first-year students finished school in the summer of 1979, and some of them have plans for restoring old farms. Forty applications were received for the second year and 18 applicants were admitted.

The school is led by a teacher who recruits instructors as needed from the local population. The teacher says of them: 'They often achieve excellent results through interaction with young people. They are in fact experts in fields which nowadays are called by fine-sounding names: aquaculture, freshwater biology, forestry, mussel-cultivation. . . .' Any more theoretical material which might be needed is covered by correspondence courses.

Future prospects for this type of 'pioneer' school are many – it may for example be linked to livelihoods threatened with extinction, or qualify unemployed under twenties to earn a living in depopulated areas. In terms of education it exemplifies the old precept that young people learn by doing.

An old boat; a farm smithy; a mill.

This is an example of how teachers and pupils at Vartdal school (Ørsta, Norway) used the optional subject hours in the seventh, eighth and ninth forms (grades).

The idea came into being on the teachers' study day in the spring of 1977, when several teachers agreed to look for work assignments outside the school. The school had already used material from the local community in its teaching; however, without arousing much interest among the pupils. Those classified as 'tired of school' had been particularly passive. The teachers expressed a wish to bring their classes *out* of school and into the local environment.

The teachers made enquiries locally and found a rare old boat rotting away, a farm blacksmith's workshop in disuse, and a 200-year-old grain mill which had been partly restored by a local farmer.

The boat was restored by the ninth form with the help of one or two teachers. They scraped, sandpapered, tarred, riveted, replaced the keel, made a new rudder, cut out and sewed new sails at school. Pupils were helped by advice from the Sunnmøre Museum. In the spring the boat was ready to be launched, and in the middle of their examination preparations the pupils relaxed with a sailing trip on the fjord.

The smithy proved to be in such a state of decay that it had to be pulled down, but the smith's forge, of stone, and much of the technical equipment was in order. A seventh-form class devised a three-year plan: they would restore the smithy as an exact replica of the original. Before pulling it down they took exact measurements and photographs, studied a number of old architectural details, planned how to get hold of materials in the same way as the original builders had done, etc. In the autumn of 1978 work was delayed by rain, but the pupils did not give up. Their teacher is a competent carpenter and planned a number of activities involving carpentry for them. The work was completed in 1981.

Part of *the mill* has been restored in 1970, especially the building itself and the equipment. However, the 400-metre-long channel and water pipes were in a poor state. The pupils decided to clean up and repair the channel system, with the aim of making it possible for the mill to be used again. The ninth-form pupils discussed the use of tools and equipment and organized themselves into work teams. All work had to be done by hand. The class spent three to four hours a week on the task, but had to bring in help from other forms. Parallel with the purely physical labour, the class studied the technical machinery and made this at the school. The pupils also researched the historical background: the sheer physical effort which had been needed for survival in earlier times, the importance of having enough water to run the mill, etc. A farmer acted as adviser and 'teaching auxiliary'. And one beautiful day in May, when thawing snow had filled the river, the sluice gates were opened and the mill wheels started to turn!

The teachers report many positive reactions in the village, including the allocation of funds from the cultural budget. The projects greatly improved pupils' attitudes and enthusiasm, especially among pupils who were weak in theoretical subjects. Teacher/pupil relationships became much more informal, and mutual understanding improved.[13]

Discussion.

The four projects discussed in this section have come into being in different ways. The Director of Education has administrative authority, but has exercised this authority in the form of discussions, stimulation, suggested ideas, development of materials, information, liaison work etc. The University has no administrative authority over schools and was forced to work in much the same way as the Director. At Vartdal School some of the teachers, through their own interest, started something which no one, in fact, could stop them from doing: teaching projects for optional subject hours in secondary school. The pioneer school presumably originated from ideas connected with conservation, and the idea was picked up and developed by the Folk University, an organization experienced in unconventional organization of adult education. In all four cases it would seem that the basic ideas are given concrete form before the pupils come into the picture.

The teachers have given strong priority to awakening their pupils' interest for the ideas and plans they have developed. This phase has probably been decisive – nothing would have been achieved or even started without the pupils' interest and participation. Pupil-activity and initiative during project work seems to have been considerable.

Social participation – the solving of particular working problems – has hardly been the main aim. For the teachers, learning has been the point, and they have chosen work assignments accordingly. But both cultural conservation and economic self-sufficiency, through exploitation of resources in arctic areas, are also socially meaningful.

Critical evaluation of project activity should be assured by teacher participation. Knowledge and experience from the projects should also be easily incorporated into school subjects in secondary schools, but the national test and examination systems make pupils' interest in local matters an open question.

In the cases where the teacher has brought material from the local community – such as leaflets on local history – teacher and pupil roles have hardly been changed. But when pupils and teachers have gone out together to observe and solve practical problems, the distance between the teachers and pupils has been reduced. The teacher's role becomes one of preparing the ground, making contacts, seeking expertise, while in the actual learning/work process he or she seems to function as a participant on the same reflective basis as the pupils.

It seems clear that locally-orientated activity in secondary schools has led to improved contact between the school and its environment. There are also clear examples to show that the school is experienced by the pupils as useful, rather than just a place for young people to go to. It seems clear, too, that varied activity in the local environment has a positive effect on weaker pupils. This may be partly because they are given the opportunity to go on building up something they can master and are familiar with, and partly because they are able to practise practical skills.

Improved learning

We have described examples in which the starting point has been a specific problem – young people with difficulties at school, or the school's isolation from the local community. In the following examples, the intention seems to be to lean towards a more general improvement in pupils' learning. Strong emphasis is placed on assuring the pupils' motivation and involvement, on activity in groups and individual cases, and on actual experience and research.

The Young People's Town (Copenhagen).

The Young People's Town is part of the State Educational Research Centre. The Town has a number of buildings paid for and run by various institutions and organizations. The buildings were put up by apprentices in various building trades as part of their training. A number of young artists have contributed decorative work. At the present time the Town offers one-day socially-orientated courses (for the eighth to the tenth grades) in the following buildings: a bank, an insurance company, a post office, a town hall, a savings bank, and a computer centre. Each course lasts about five hours, and is held, apart from the group reception, in one building throughout.

Each course starts out from a familiar situation, aiming, through various teaching methods, to give young people insight into some aspect of family and society, as a supplement to their learning in schools.

The course-instructors are experts from the various fields represented in the Town. The teaching is planned in close co-operation with teachers from the Educational Research Centre, and the programmes often function as models for similar courses elsewhere in Denmark.

The course users – teachers and students – constantly evaluate the method and content of the courses with the help of questionnaires which are filled in after a visit to the Town. This constant supply of 'customer feedback' plays an important part in the continual revision of the courses.[14]

Open assignment situations

The Work Research Institute in Oslo was originally created to provide alternative structures for organization and management in industry. The Institute has, however, also been involved in educational projects. The starting-point has been a study of organization and work structure. A general distinction is made between two structures: the *production model*, in which starting-point, material, method/operation and result/product are given, and the *research model*, in which only the starting point/problem is given while both method and result are open.[15]

Research workers at the WRI soon observed that the production model is widely used in schools: subjects are split up into small isolated pieces which the pupils study and learn, one at a time. They must follow rigid instructions, and achievement is judged high or low on both results achieved and on ability to follow instructions.

In contrast to this, the WRI has devised the research model or the *open assignment situation*: students are given the freedom to investigate, discuss and find out things on their own. Activity is problem-orientated and the teacher's role is defined as being that of a resource person. If drill is necessary for learning, the process will show when and why. Achievement is not exclusively evaluated as right or wrong, but is seen in relation to increased competence and possibility for further research. The WRI has made intensive studies of teaching in Norway and Sweden, and has led a number of projects in technical and mercantile schools, high schools and colleges of education.

Pupils as researchers (Norway).

A vocational school in a Norwegian industrial town started an extra-year course in industrial electronics. The teacher worked out a plan of the fields to be covered: basic concepts in maths and physics, technical literature to be read in English, practice of already familiar theory, familiarization with industry through concrete co-operation projects, and, most important, practical vocational skills and theory. However, the plan described very little about how the pupils should work.

Much of the work covered in the assignments comes directly from the local industrial environment, e.g. electronic surveillance of greenhouses, (including temperature reading), transfer from hydraulic to electronic systems in mechanical industry, finding the right condensation level of a herring-oil factory, finding ways of saving electricity in a foundry, providing an adjustable, recorded organ accompaniment for hymn-singing in a chapel with no organist.

The pupils work on problems individually or in groups, contact the different concerns and consult experts. The teacher supervises, helps, discusses possible solutions, etc.

The *teaching* provided is tailored to the projects in hand and the pupils' need. The rest of the teacher's time is spent on planning and outside contact with industrial and vocational interests.

Evaluation of the work is primarily through continual discussion. For the examination, the candidate must appear in front of a test committee to describe and discuss the work he or she has been doing.

Six years after work was begun, these working principles are now being transferred to a new line in the vocational school. A survey shows that pupils from this electronics line do well in their careers and earn good salaries.[16]

The schools of Tvind (Denmark).

The first of the several schools of Tvind was started in 1970 as a travelling folk high school, and the movement now includes an alternative compulsory school for those in the 14 to 17 age-group (Efterskole) and a four-year teacher-training programme which is recognized by the Ministry of Education.

The schools came into existence because Denmark's laws and traditions enable the State to cover 85 per cent of the running expenses of the private schools.

In Tvind (a little place on the coast of West Jutland) new dimensions are being given to teacher/pupil roles and new ways are being found of describing what knowledge is, and how learning and socialization can be carried out. Years of experience and many discussions have led to the following statement of educational principles:[17]

1. You must go out and explore in order to make new concepts for yourself, and on further exploration to improve on those concepts;

2. You must get on intimate terms with things you want to learn about; the closer you get, the more you will learn;

3. You and your fellow students must be the driving force in your efforts to learn; life is too important to rely on the teacher's tricks to get you going;

4. You must learn that the more you start, the more you will finish; the deeper you look into problems, the more you will learn; it means hard work – but at least you will not be superficial or apathetic;

5. You can't learn everything at school, but only the top of the iceberg; the rest comes later;

6. Only Adam was alone in the world. The rest of us are here together;

7. What you learn is meant to be used, and preferably now, so that others can learn from you, but possibly also later, if the opportunity arises; you learn twice as well by passing things on to someone else;

8. You must be able to move about, so that you experience as much as possible; otherwise, everything will be at a standstill. Even if you have periscope eyes, the view from one spot is restricted.

9. Everything said here also applies to teachers.

The teachers draw up the main lines for each course (an example might be five months of practical and theoretical studies, four months of travelling by bus, one month of follow-up). Within this framework, each course is self-administrating, with a meeting of all students and teachers as the highest authority. Meetings decide such matters as study programmes, finances, internal issues, etc. At meetings, students and teachers have equal status. There is no vote; discussions go on until agreement is reached.

The Tvind schools have no daily or weekly timetable. All work schedules are decided by the group. A visitor reports that the only difference between weekdays and weekends is that there are far more visitors at weekends.

Students and teachers have built the schools themselves. A large complex now exists, including residential buildings, workshops, farm buildings, a windmill, and a solar energy unit. Almost all work is carried out by students and teachers, including office work, cooking, farming, maintenance, cleaning, printing, transportation, bus maintenance, looking after visitors, etc.

This system of organization, decision-making and practical work helps the student to learn:

1. to structure his or her own working day;
2. to make his or her own situation for learning;
3. to become involved in making the conditions for his or her own existence.

As an illustration we will quote from a report on one of Tvind's Projects.

Pre-feudal slavery: history for the ninth grade

'At the start of the year, the grade had a history week. It started with a discussion on how history could be learnt, because history is usually perceived as a boring subject, where the students sit and plough through book after book on sun kings and various royal balls and diversions, without getting to know anything at all about the people who had to stand on the firing line when things went wrong. And yet, most of the people are common, ordinary folk, like most of the students. The students finally decided to make a historical film about former societies: the primitive age, the age of slavery, and the feudal age.'

This is a report on the age of slavery and on making a film: 'After the meeting, the students split up into 3 groups, each covering one age. The one group started by listening to a lecture on slavery for two or three hours. Then they split into smaller groups: one group were craftsmen, the second was to make clothes, and the third was to find wood. Finally, there was a group to do anything else that was necessary. When everything was ready, the students repaired an old bus, loaded it up, and went off to various historical places. Of course, every filming scene had to be rehearsed a lot. But the first shots were of the surroundings the peasants and Vikings lived in, so that the actors could get an idea of what it was like to live at that time.'

'Then the group demonstrated how they worked and what they worked with, and finally the group gave the film a plot. When it was all done, the group went home and developed the film, cut it and added the soundtrack. The other groups went through a similar process. Finally, all the films were shown at a get-together in the evening, and they were a great success.'

Larvic Technical College

Students from the college's advanced course (part 1 in welding and construction) have since 1974 had three days a week at the foundry of Alfr. Anderson Ltd. and two days a week of theoretical instruction at the college. The foundry employs 350 and is very close to the college. The arrangement was made after the former head of the college approached the industrial association in Larvik. The firm showed immediate interest.

In the practical part of the course students follow the foundry routine and do productive work from the firm's own drawings and instructions. We constantly try to find work assignments connected with the teaching syllabus in welding and construction. The college instructor is responsible for the whole course, and he spends the three days of practical work at the foundry with the students:

'For the first three years the foundry provided an adviser who helped the college students by providing drawings, materials, machines and other equipment. He was also responsible for checking and accepting the work done. Later the college teacher was responsible for the day-to-day work, while the foundry foreman provided work assignments and checked the finished products. The foreman comes to the shed where the students work several times a week. He checks the work and the work processes, and talks to the students and their teacher. The students ask him and other workmen questions just as they ask their teacher. Three or four times a year the foreman comes to the school and talks to the students on subjects the teacher wants to take up in the class. . .

In theory classes the drawings to be used in the foundry are gone through, in an attempt to integrate theory and practical work. . .

Before every assignment the students discuss the best way of approaching and carrying out the work among themselves, and then show their suggestions to the teachers, who agree or suggest changes.

The students are paid apprentice rates. Many continue on apprentice contracts the following year and go on to take a trade certificate. . .

Results have been extremely positive. Students, college and foundry are all satisfied. Co-operation with the foundry, from the director down to the shop floor, is an example for others to follow. There is no sign that this relationship will not continue to flourish. One of the union stewards at the foundry said recently that these boys are so important for recruitment that the firm would probably go a long way to keep the arrangement.'

(Report from inspector of studies Erik Olaussen.)

NAF (the Norwegian Employers Association) has published an interview with the project leader and others. We quote some views:

It's nice to watch the students at work here. . . . I hardly recognize them from the first year basic course. Before they were a bit sulky and hard to talk to. Now they talk openly, meet my eyes, and discuss the work. The boys like to be worked hard, but they have to have a say in things. I try to get them to think from the management's point of view so they realise they have the opportunity to suggest changes.

(Teacher Ivan Næss)

As long as these are fulfilled, we are happy, and we think the college is too. . . . The students must follow our working regulations, come and go at set times and work a full day. They know they are part of a production process which is no longer a game but a serious matter. We are responsible for the finished products. We check that the welding and construction have been carried out properly. Our margins are narrow. Time is also an important factor. The work must be done quickly and effectively, never better nor worse than the customer or Norwegian standard require.

(Foreman K.S. Husene, on work requirements)

This used to be a difficult area. Training students or apprentices requires independent working assignments and expert instructors. It does not matter that much who does the job. The advantage of our set-up with Larvik technical college is that Næss is an expert technician and supervisor who can spend all his time with the students while they are here. . . . Apprentices, and students out in working practice, are often left to workers who have little idea of how to teach others. The bosses, and skilled workers too, often used to go around with the drawings in their pocket. No-one was allowed to look at them. They wouldn't 'let-slip' any knowledge. They could build a whole bridge without letting anyone else see a drawing! Their way of doing things was to give orders: do this and do that. We have had to teach them to let other people share their drawings and their expertise. The introduction of democracy on the shop floor has improved learning and given better opportunities for activity and participation.

(Foreman Husene, on supervision of students and apprentices)

In theory lessons we get straight to the point because we have the foundry drawings for the work we are going to carry out. The drawings are broken down and gone through at the college. In this way the students become familiar with the technical symbols and terms they have to know in order to work from drawings. Here we have a great advantage over students in other professions, who do many pieces of practical work at college with barely any training in 'reading' drawings.

(Teacher Næss)

The students have no feeling of 'going to school', and this has a noticeable effect on their attitude to work assignments at the foundry. On the basic course at the college, on the other hand, we made things which had no practical value, and it was a bit depressing to make things you knew were going to be thrown away.

(Student representative Bjørn Ekvall)

1978-9 was a difficult year for the industry. This affected the supply work assignments for the students at the foundry. Because of this situation we had to try to find commissions of our own, so that we weren't taking work away from the foundry workers. Then Næss, who is an 'agriculturalist', began to wonder if the students themselves could get orders for the foundry. The result was that teacher and students constructed and costed the production of implements for agricultural use. Costing was worked out by students in theory lessons, and the foundry calculated sufficient profit to cover expenses. It was a very successful theory assignment, which was actually put into production. The products were sold to customers through a retailer in Larvik.

Discussion.

The Young People's Town can be seen as a limited teaching aid for schools, though more concrete than other teaching aids such as film.

Both the schools connected to the Work Research Institute and the Tvind schools work with the same areas of knowledge as ordinary schools. The difference is mainly in the far more open starting point for learning; the pupils must decide for themselves how a problem is to be approached, what experience they wish to seek, and which method, work form and way of life to choose. But some guideline to methods is indicated in the schools' basic statements of purpose: the first Tvind school is called the Travelling Folk High School, and the *bus* seems to have as much importance as the classical teacher's cane. The pupils have considerable influence on the actual learning and work processes. Apart from this, there are clear differences between the WRI and Tvind: while the WRI seeks to change the learning process within the existing school framework, the Tvind people build new schools and decide the framework themselves.

In these three examples participation in society is important. In The Young People's Town the social situations experienced are mostly simulation, but this must be accepted in cases where realistic practice is difficult to arrange, as in the bank situation. For Tvind it is important that the school itself is a society in miniature, in which the satisfaction of basic needs such as housing, food, clothes, hygiene, and communication are connected closely to the teaching and social function.

In the WRI's electronics class work assignments, to a large degree, are decided by problems and observations within the industries concerned. The pupils' ultimate aim is a vocational qualification; otherwise at times it would be difficult to distinguish between learning and work.

At Larvik Technical College the realistic working situation seems to be the key to effective learning. Here the requirements of 'the customer or the Norwegian Standard' must be fulfilled. But although the work has to be done to schedule, the students obviously have more time than the foundry workers. It is also interesting to notice that teacher and students together developed a useful, saleable product when the foundry was short of orders.

Critical reflection seems to be ensured in all the four examples, partly through the teacher's presence, partly through organization of experiences and the possibility of group discussions. There seems also to be a clear connection between experiences and searching for the practical or theoretical knowledge needed to carry out the tasks. If the students do not try to find things out for themselves, the teacher is able to make them. In all the examples the students see that they can obtain information from different adults and not only from books. At Larvik Technical College, according to the report, more emphasis is placed on the course teaching than on project work; but this teaching is closely linked with work assignments. This seems to be the key to the interesting co-operation between college and workshop, and probably explains the positive change of attitude of the students from the first to the second year.

Pupil and teacher roles are radically changed. When Tvind schools state that *the same pedagogical principles apply to both pupils and teachers*, something significant is being said. Part of the change is probably due to the use of practical activity, which also has to be learnt, even in theoretical subjects. The Tvind schools, therefore, seem to give the whole person a chance to succeed, through the reciprocal action of theoretical and practical skills.

The activities described in these examples seem, without doubt, to have led to better learning.

LBP principles: a challenge to Scandinavia

The examples given in this chapter have described attempts to solve problems for adolescents with difficulties at school, to integrate the school into the local social environment, and generally to improve pupils' learning. All the examples seem to show that the principles of pupil influence and social participation have given encouraging results. Further, the best results seem to be achieved in cases where practical experience is evaluated through critical reflection, and the result integrated into *wider* areas of knowledge.

The following examples seem to correspond most closely to LBP principles: Åbak Efterskole, Veslestua, subject options at Vartdal school, the Pioneer school, the electronic class, and Latvik Technical College. The results also appear to be best in these cases. The starting point in these examples is important: *pupils and teachers start out together in an open situation, in which they can and must make decisions themselves*. In practice this means that they have freed themselves from standardized administrative regulations within the school system, such as timetables, syllabus descriptions, methods, etc.

We have already pointed out that the political democracy in Scandinavia has achieved a great deal as regards equal educational opportunities for all, schools as meeting places for all social groups, and equal and stable economic conditions for all schools. These must remain educational aims. But when we look at the content and the learning situations in schools, we see that the standardized systems, enforced by administrators, invalidate the democratic reality for pupils and teachers in their daily activities. Everyone may exert democratic influence upon larger issues, which are discussed in the

government and parliament, but important decisions about pupils'
and teachers' daily work are made above them in the hierarchy.

New standardization factors in the system

A look at the present tendencies in schools, and the encouraging
results achieved with LBP principles, suggests that the root of the
present crisis lies in the standardization of learning situations and
content. Of course, these regulating factors cannot simply be
abandoned. A central principle in a political democracy is the fair
distribution of advantages and opportunities. The question the
school must answer now is: what are the actual advantages of
education, and where are concrete changes needed?

Bearing LBP principles in mind, it seems reasonable to discuss
standardization or regulation in the following areas:

1. *All children and young people should be given the same amount of
   time for learning.* The time available should not be measured in
   teaching hours, but, more flexibly, in years and possibly in
   working weeks. It must be a public responsibility to ensure that
   the financial needs of all children and young people are available
   so that adequate time can actually be spent on learning.
2. *A teacher/pupil ratio must be established (e.g. 1:15), which will
   ensure a sufficient number of teachers at all schools.* In the course of
   LBP project work, a teacher role seems to be developing in which
   the central functions are to prepare the ground for project work,
   to work with the pupils, to relate work to critical reflection and a
   more general context, and to stimulate pupils towards group
   activity. Much of the teacher's time must be spent on discussing
   work with smaller groups or individual pupils. Thus the
   pupil/teacher ratio is very important. It appears advisable that
   the present standard class sizes, determined by law, should be
   dropped, and the organization of pupils into appropriate units
   be left to each school.
3. *Buildings and equipment must become more flexible.* The present
   school system is rooted in conventional concepts of class sizes,
   teaching, discipline, etc. It is important to formulate rules which
   will allow flexible learning and social situations.
4. *Funds must be made available for out-of-school experiences.* There

is a lot to learn outside the classroom. Field trips to provide experience and observations should not be considered as light relief, but as an obvious and essential part of school work.

5. *Opportunities and challenges must be made available for social participation.* LBP project work indicates the necessity of drawing schools into the local environment. The local community ought to be able to draw on the school's resources, both in work on essential problems and in considering what might be desirable in the future. Environmental and cultural conservation often lack funds, and certain goods or services are not available because they are incompatible with profit-making, etc.

If we choose to standardize the school system in these or similar ways, we shall, in fact, be preparing the ground for the use of LBP principles. This will also involve new tasks for the administrators, though it would, in fact, seem preferable for teachers and pupils to be responsible for the administration which most directly involves them. Here too are important possibilities for learning and social contact.

Lack of necessary knowledge in schools

We have described examples of LBP in practice. The results have proved good or promising, and we have also discussed necessary changes in the school's system and organization. In my opinion, this is still not enough to enable LBP principles to be introduced all over in Scandinavia. In several of the examples described it was clear that teachers have problems with their own, their colleagues' and their administrators' knowledge of central educational conditions: learning, socialization, forms of knowledge, teaching, social training, organization of pupils and material, the school's aims, the school's relation to society and culture, evaluation, and pupil and teacher roles. I believe it is essential for Scandinavian educators to admit that they possess *a general lack of basic knowledge and skills at all levels of the school system.*

One explanation of this lies in Scandinavian teacher-training: demands on teachers' qualifications have mainly been limited to knowledge of school subjects and the question of how to teach them. A grounding in the basic pedagogical points mentioned above has never been considered necessary and has not been made possible.

Two examples from the European school tradition may cast light on the usual attitudes towards teacher qualifications: Rektor Adolf Diesterweg (1790—1866) was removed from his position as head of the teachers' seminary in Berlin in 1847 because he gave teachers too thorough a training. The authorities then removed subjects which gave 'a wider horizon' (pedagogics, psychology, anthropology, literary history and world history) from the seminary's teaching.[18] The Minister of Education in Norway in 1931 wanted to reduce teacher-training from two years to one, because teaching ability was considered to be a gift of God rather than a product of professional training.[19]

Teacher-training has long been from one-third to one-half of the length of training of doctors, theologians or lawyers, or roughly the same length as that of lower military officers. Teacher-training has never been an important political issue in Scandinavia, and there has been little incentive to use adequate resources. This is probably connected with the widespread opinion that the training of teachers is really impossible or unnecessary.

Scandinavian colleges of education, for a long time, were tied to the Lutheran state churches, and religion was the main subject. In correspondence with the religious way of thinking which was centred on the individual, training colleges also taught behaviourist psychology, and history of schools. Little time has been given to the study of schools and educational thinking in other countries. Scandinavians have, to some extent justifiably, been accused of being so satisfied with their own schools that they consider it unnecessary to know anything about schools in other countries!

The Scandinavian universities also share the blame for inadequate teacher-qualifications. The universities have placed most emphasis on a lengthy course in traditional high school subjects, followed by a final short course in psychology, history of schools, instructional methods, and teaching practice. Institutes of education have also been firmly based on positivistic thought and behaviourist psychology. Their contribution to schools has, therefore, mainly taken the form of methods of evaluation and testing, and of didactics and methods based on principles of teaching technology.

Against this background, I think it is natural that teachers interested in LBP have problems with their own, their colleagues' and their administration's insight into critical educational points. A teacher confronted with the present crisis in schools, needs insight into a number of scientific disciplines: philosophy, sociology, psychology of the individual and psychology of groups, anthropology, economics, theory of organization, history, didactics and methods. Development – i.e., the gaining of new insights – within these disciplines has been very rapid during the last two decades. However, new insights are still weak in the school system.

The main problem in teacher education is the lack of coordination between theory and practice. Subject studies at the colleges of education seem isolated or hardly relevant to teaching practice. Attempts are now being made to solve this problem by linking the two areas into 'educational theory and practice', and the increase of teaching hours from half a year to one year altogether, with the three year course. But teaching in different subjects and fields can still go on independent of teaching practice. This split is further widened by the organization of tutors at colleges of education into subject departments, rather than, for instance, teaching groups for each year-group of students. Practice teachers (Teaching supervisors) are basically employees of the state school system, while subject tutors rarely have the opportunity to follow their students during teaching practice.

In the education of teachers the LBP model could solve a number of problems connected with the split between theory and practice. The model could be sketched like this:

Figure 4.

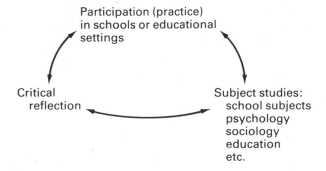

The model requires subject-theory tutors to follow the students in teaching practice and/or the practice supervisors to have a general idea of the subject teaching at the college. All teachers must share responsibility for critical assessment, reflection, discussion of problem areas, generalizations etc. But as student groups gain insight into the LBP-model, and perhaps also see that it works, they will probably take over much of the responsibility for carrying out all stages of the process.

A new opportunity for practical educationalists and theorists

During the first post-war period (1945—65) politicians had their time of opportunity. There was strong agreement about the desirability of education, the importance of equal educational opportunities for all, and the need to build schools all over the country. The building of new schools would also promote economic growth. There was no serious opposition to the rapid expansion of the educational system.

In the years 1965—1975 serious concern began to be expressed inside all the fine buildings. A number of *technical* changes were tried, such as AV equipment, pre-fabricated teaching programmes, octagonal school buildings, schools without walls (open-plan schools), and more administrative posts. At the same time surveys show that a number of pupils learn very little in their last years at school, and in some cases it has been found that school is a place where they do *not* learn.

Given this state of affairs, it is clear that we cannot go on increasing the time spent at school and giving everyone still more of conventional schooling. This is a dilemma for central school politicians and administrators whose entire activity, prestige and careers have been in connection with expansion. In its own way, this is admirable, but when faced with today's crisis, their prestige is worth little; they are without insight into basic conditions.

From the examples referred to and discussed in this chapter, I would maintain that the 1980's are developing into a time for *practical educationalists and theorists*. In order to gain insight into basic educational problems, we need both the experience of bold innovators (as at the schools in Tvind and Vartdal) and the insight of educational theorists well schooled in social studies and related disciplines. The following recommendations are proposed:

1. Trust must be placed in teachers. They must be given the opportunity to try LBP projects.
2. Basic educational factors such as learning, socialization, forms of knowledge, teaching, organization, etc., must be analysed with a view to developing new principles.
3. General information on educational questions must be made available, with the aim of giving people and politicians enough insight to be able to take part in educational development again.

Notes and References

1. DALIN, P. and SKRINDO, M. (Eds) (1981). *Laering ved deltaking*. Ungdom i skole og arbeidsliv. Universitetsforlaget Oslo, p. 121.
2. Sources of information regarding colleges/universities are: Roskilde Universitets-Center (RUC), Denmark; Sosialpedagogisk Studiealternativ, Universitet i Oslo; Oppland Distriktshøgskole, Lillehammer and Statens Spesiallaererhøgskole, Oslo. At Halden College of Education, Norway, Per Linge and Hans Petter Wille are leading a project on 'Work for Children in Kindergartens' (Linge and Wille, 1980). A number of schools have camp-schools programmes.
3. Sources of information regarding projects in Scandinavia can be obtained from the IMTEC office in Oslo and from the Norsk Pedagogisk Studiesamling, University Library, Oslo. There are a number of special reports.
4. SKRINDO, M. (1978 and 1981). 'Vil vi karakterer – likevel?', *Forskningsnytt*, 3/1978, and 'Normerte prøver i norsk – hvilke mål fremmer de?', *Norsklaereren*, 4/1981.
5. MELLIN-OLSEN, S. and RASMUSSEN, R. (1975). *Skolens vold*. Pax, Oslo. And MONSEN, L. (Ed) (1978). *Kunnskapssosiologi og skoleutvikling*. Universitetsforlaget, Oslo.
6. See brochures and reports available on request from the National Council for Innovation in Education Project, Forsøksradet, Oslo.
7. FORSØKSRÅDET FOR SKOLEVERKET (1981). *Utvida opplæring*. Rapport om forsøket Alternativ oppkæring 1974-79, Oslo 1980. Samarbeid mellom den videregående skolen og arbeidslivet, Oslo.
8. STOUGAARD, V. (1979). *Aabæk Efterskole*. København.
9. KRISTOFFERSEN, K. and WESTBY O. (1979). *Veslestua skole*. Oslo: NKS-forlaget.
10. Ibid.
11. ALEXANDERSEN, I. (1979). 'Lokalsamfunnet i skolen. Pedagogisk utviklingarbeid i Finnmark', *Pedagogen*, 4/1979.
12. SOLSTAD, K.J. (1978). *Riksskole i utkantstrøk*. Oslo: Universitetsforlaget, and HØGMO, A., SOLSTAD, K.J. and TILLER, Y. (1981). *Skolen og den lokale utfordring*, Universitet i Tromsø.

13. DALIN, P. and SKRINDO, M. (Eds) (1981). *Læring ved deltaking.* Ungdom i skole og arbeidsliv. Universitetsforlaget, Oslo.
14. Further information about the course is available from Statens Padegogiske Forsøgscenter, Copenhagen, Denmark.
15. THORSRUD, E. and EMERY, F.E. (1969). *Form and Content in Industrial Democracy.* London: Tavistock Publications, and HERBST, P.G. (1973). *Socio-Technical Design.* London: Tavistock Publications.
16. BLICKFELDT, J.F., HAUGEN, R. and JANGÅRD, H. (1979). *Mot en ny skoleorganisation.* Oslo: Tanum.
17. Further information about these principles and about the schools of Tvind is available from Skipper Clement Forlag, Ulfsborg, Denmark.
18. GRUE-SØRENSEN, K. (1961). *Opdragelsens Historie III*, København, p. 155.
19. DAHL, H. (1959). *Norsk lærerutdanning*, Oslo, p. 318.

CHAPTER SIX
Towards learning by participation: an international perspective

PER DALIN

In order for any educational change to take root, a comprehensive understanding of the process of change itself is necessary. This final chapter, therefore, attempts to apply a systematic analysis of educational change to Learning By Participation. First, the chapter discusses the social, economic and educational factors that determine the need for LBP, and then examines LBP in terms of change-theory. Next, problems related to the implementation of LBP are described, as are strategies which might be employed to overcome these problems. In conclusion the author suggests directions for the future; in particular, ways in which efforts might be joined to support the further development and expansion of Learning By Participation. Per Dalin is Director of IMTEC-The International Learning Co-operative.

The purpose of this chapter is to consider issues related to the implementation of LBP in schools, looking particularly at four major spheres of concern: the major social, economic and educational motivations for implementing LBP-type programmes in schools; the consequences of implementing LBP at the individual, school and schools-systems level and discussing some of the major forces at work in society which appear to facilitate or severely limit implementation possibilities; alternative strategies educators might consider if they wish to initiate LBP programmes, discussing these strategies at the classroom, school and school system levels; and finally, we offer certain speculations as to the future of LBP in the educational enterprise.

Forces supporting Learning by Participation

We believe that any significant reform activity within the education

203

sector has its roots in a genuine sense of need, both within and outside the school. A wide range of motivations has been discussed in this book, and we should like to summarize and analyse what appear to be the major ones.

Youth-to-adult transition

In Chapter One, Dollar and Rust point to many ways in which schools and their roles in modern society fail young people. Isolating students as they do from 'real' life, even the schools' increasingly flexible curricula fail to meet young people's social and psycho-emotional needs, and the result is often dissatisfaction within the schools and unhappiness in the young people; many of the programmes examined in this study began to function with students who were school 'dropouts'.

A major point of this study is that these same young people have a valid and useful contribution to make to the world in which, after all, they live. The authors believe that Learning By Participation becomes an answer. LBP programmes can represent a last try to create a real-life 'here and now' situation that will give young people a sense of belonging, responsibility and self-respect. Although some LBP experiences are radical and demand much of the adult world, it is possible, as nearly all the cases we have presented show, to build learning programmes which involve students in a holistic sense, and which meet developmental needs at present largely ignored by traditional school curricula.

It has to be admitted, however, that LBP programmes have a tendency to be limited because they often become 'radical alterna-tives' (e.g., the schools of Tvind in Denmark); and because they are isolated alternatives, they attract special students and therefore seldom have direct impact on the curricula of the main schools.

School-to-work transition

In all countries involved in our study, it has been found that schooling poorly prepares young people for the world of work.

For those students who use secondary school as a springboard for embarking upon more advanced educational programmes, this is no great problem. The others, however, whose schooling ends when their days of compulsory education are over, are in a critical situation, facing unemployment which rises daily, and thus an increasingly competitive job market. Because of this, many young people decide to continue in school in spite of their personal desire to leave and in spite of the fact that schools often perpetuate a sense of failure and inadequacy in these particular young people.

The conclusion that must be drawn is that modern society has not managed to develop a policy for young people that can cope with both their needs and those of society. We believe that LBP opens the way towards a new strategy – that of combining school work and responsible roles in society. It also provides opportunities for work experience in a number of areas where the ordinary work force has no vested interests. It points at some alternative futures for both education and work. We do not believe that the industrialized nations will be able to continue their economic and social development without drastic redefinitions of three areas of life: work, education, and leisure. To isolate each area within its own 'box' becomes more and more artificial in an economy that is less and less work-intensive, with education that is more and more aimless, and with 'leisure' that seems to have become synonymous with consumption. Strong incentives in terms of economic compensation are linked to a narrowly defined 'productive sector' to which we belong for a shorter and shorter period of our lives, while the 'non-productive years' already occupy the largest portion of our life-time.

We are fully aware that a redefinition of productive and unproductive roles raises fundamental questions about our economies. Nevertheless, we quite often find 'non-productive' roles in leisure-time activities more useful for the individual and for society than the 'productive' roles in the work situation. We also find that learning may well take place equally well during the work period and leisure time as in the school period.

The school to work transition is somewhat conditioned by the structure of our society. Should economic and social incentives be more equally distributed between 'productive' and 'non-productive' roles, we believe that our whole life-style would change and so would attitudes toward education, work and leisure.

Learning by Participation raises fundamental questions regarding the boundaries between education, work and leisure. It is an approach to learning that breaks down some of these artificial boundaries. It does, however, also have limitations in relation to the work force:

1. In an economy where unemployment is reaching record-breaking levels, LBP might be seen as a threat to jobs;
2. Until this point LBP has been a 'bridging strategy' between school and work, assuming that the existing boundaries and separation of tasks remain. We do not believe that the *fundamental* question of the separation of an increasing proportion of young people (and the workforce in general) from productive roles can be resolved through LBP. In fact, LBP might simply delay the basic question of a redefinition of 'productive' versus 'non-productive' roles and thereby the redistribution of incentives.

School curriculum reform

The tendency of schools to become isolated islands in society means that they often present a distorted view of the realities of life. Sometimes this distortion has to do with a curriculum in favour of a 'national culture' representing an 'urban white middle-class elite' view which ignores or misrepresents the life of local communities. In other cases the voices of minority groups are not heard and the needs of their children are forgotten. It is impossible for education to be value-free; which values, then, and what interest-groups, will be served by an increasingly comprehensive school?

The choice is often a 'neutral' curriculum and a non-committed teacher. There is nothing more boring to young people who need to identify themselves with adults as well as with causes they can believe in, and nothing does them greater disservice than such neutral choices. The result is not only boredom, but a school that increasingly isolates itself from contemporary society with its dynamic interplay of social and economic forces.

Several LBP programmes reported in this volume are a response to schools that have isolated themselves from society. The programmes reflect the needs of young people as well as those of teachers who find LBP programmes 'a new beginning' for themselves as teachers.

Schooling has become too theoretical. European countries which have undergone a transition from a tripartite school system towards comprehensive schooling have found that they have not fully understood the consequences of bringing the whole age-range into one school. The old *real-schule* with its academic emphasis has often survived the structural changes, the result being a mismatch between the curriculum and student needs. We believe that LBP offers a new beginning for uninterested learners. Several of the cases in this book illustrate the 'energy-mobilizer effect' that LBP programmes have.

LBP, however, goes beyond a simple expansion of curriculum choices. It redefines roles and responsibilities within the school curriculum. While traditional school programmes have a tendency to foster passivity and prolong dependency, by contrast LBP creates and implements curricula through a shared responsibility of both learners and teachers. In other words, LBP is also a curriculum *process* reform.

We have seen that different countries react in different ways to LBP experiments. While some seem to encourage and facilitate school-based reforms, other countries appear to need a central mandate to enable schools to develop LBP (e.g., the Netherlands and, in part, Norway). It seems that LBP cannot be packaged: although a number of ideas and materials can be developed centrally, the quality and success of LBP rests with the learners, the teachers, and the local school support. When the system, in other words, plays such an important role, LBP raises fundamental questions of system reform.

System reform

The breakdown of hierarchical control towards local initiative and responsibility is a major departure from traditional school reform. It represents a double departure, from both the traditional European school system and from the comprehensive school. This school was seen as a vehicle to take us towards educational and social equality. Because of it, the school organization and the curriculum were standardized, no difficult task as central bureaucratic control of the school was already a tradition into which the standardization of the comprehensive school fitted relatively easily. In fact, the famous expression 'The more things change, the more they remain the same' can easily be applied to comprehensive school development, at least when it comes to policy-making, management, and control.

We have already pointed out the dangers of nationally standardized curricula and the increasing awareness that the comprehensive school represents an urban, industrialized, 'modern' society which leaves little room for alternative cultures and lifestyles. We believe that LBP programmes become a resource for the local community. They bring the school back from its isolation from that community, and bring the students into the community, so that they become a present, and in all probability a future resource. Many communities have experienced the departure of their young people following the introduction of prolonged compulsory schooling. There are few points of identification with the community, and the young people head for the attraction of an urban setting. LBP is seen by many local communities as a resource to build identification with the community.

The question of equality of educational opportunities remains unanswered. Is it possible that too great a freedom for the local community – indeed for the individual teacher – will create an unnecessary imbalance? Decentralization has been, and could still be, an excuse for an unequal quality of provision for rich and poor communities. LBP programmes could also be used to widen the gap between the 'haves' and the 'have-nots'. What critics seldom see, however, is that the existing standardized curricula favour the urban setting. In fact communities can differ substantially and to treat them as if they were the same is the best guarantee for true inequality. Student motivation and identification with the curricula is a precondition for learning. By giving each local setting the freedom to create its own programmes, LBP can provide such preconditions. To ensure that inequality does not develop further, however, central authorities need to ensure equal access to financial resources, access which is already established in several countries.

The Dutch Innovation Committee for Learning by Participation is the best example of a national initiative to restructure the school system along LBP-principles. Holland, having a tripartite educational system split between a number of specialized schools, has so far experienced slow progress towards a more unified system. It seems, then, that the motivation for LBP and the strategy to develop it should be viewed together.

While most centralistic change-strategies leave little initiative at the local level, the Dutch Committee, realizing the importance of local motivation, has created a unique combination of central and local mobilization. There are obvious dangers: the experiment might lead to another form of standardization and central control that could hinder a continuous development process.

There is another dimension of system reform that so far has not materialized in any of the countries in this study: the integration of different youth-serving sectors, such as, for example, the schools, job-training schemes, service agencies and leisure-time activities. The best example of a tendency towards a more unified policy for young people is to be found in our cases from the USA; in most countries such a policy does not exist. Moreover, the agencies which are supposed to be working for young people often have different approaches, seldom even talking to each other, split as they are by bureaucratic structures and regulations.

To be effective, Learning by Participation needs to be a common concern for all youth-serving agencies, not seen only as a separate programme for the schools. As the 'problems of youth' are identified through the work of many agencies, the need for a coherent youth policy becomes evident. LBP might serve as a vehicle towards fulfilling this need.

Young people as a resource

Young people are often treated as a 'problem', falling between two stools and being regarded neither as children nor as full adults. As we hope our study makes plain, we believe that there is a fundamental under-utilization of adolescent potential in most industrialized countries, and that young people can make a contribution now. This is true at the community level as well as at the national level. However, perhaps because of this tendency to view young people as a problem, motivation for LBP more often grows from a desire to solve this 'problem' rather than to utilize a potential. As we suggest in earlier paragraphs, it is in the absence of a meaningful youth policy that can serve both young people and society that LBP is seen as a strategy. Even though young people are seldom considered as an 'untapped resource', in those situations where they have proved their abilities, motivation to build on their potential is evident. We suggest that LBP motivations, therefore, might begin as an attempted solution to an existing problem, and end up as a major contribution to community and national development.

Learning by Participation – implications for actors

We have defined Learning by Participation as an 'integrative process that includes participation in society, critical reflection on that participation, and the relation of experiences to theoretical knowledge, while maximizing the participation of all learners in decision-making affecting both the programmes as a whole and their own individual activities in the programme' (see Dollar and Rust, Chapter One).

To what extent are these ideals actually reflected in the programmes presented in this volume? We have earlier noted that our definition is to be looked upon as an ideal and that few programmes meet all the criteria. What is the reality for the actors involved?

THE STUDENT:
LBP means a fundamental role change for the student. He is used to a somewhat passive learning situation where adults have pre-programmed his day, where both the content as well as the method of instruction is determined by others. To what extent do students in LBP actually take on a different role?

Most programmes are successful in providing students with options – or a wider choice. They are also successful in providing students with actual, responsible, roles. What seems to be lacking in most programmes, however, is active student participation *in the planning process*. Most programmes are prepared by adults. Students are presented with options. These, however, are most often *provided* by adults. The reality of schooling is that it is adult-governed, reflects adult interest groups, and thereby often limits the possibilities for student decision-making. In addition, however, the situation is also caused by the lack of continuity of students in educational programmes.

The structure of most school curricula directs students to a number of rather isolated subject-oriented experiences throughout the school year. A teacher and a student might know each other only for the period of a course or a semester. The structure does not lend itself to responsible student roles in planning and decision-making.

Nevertheless most LBP programmes change student roles and the relationships between students and adults drastically. As Skrindo notes, 'when pupils and teachers have gone out together to observe and solve practical problems, the distance between teacher and pupil roles has been reduced'.

A common outcome in all projects described is student enthusiasm for the programme. This is as much the case for the school drop-out in Amsterdam as for the science graduate in the historical preservation project in Boston. Student participation in real-life situations that are meaningful and important both to students and society has an important consequence: students learn, and want to learn more.

THE TEACHER:

Most programmes create a new and daunting situation for the teacher. The source of information is no longer the textbook alone; in many cases other adults play a significant role as information givers. The teacher is faced with a 'curriculum' not yet described by anyone. She or he faces problems, rather than the well-organized subject matter for which she or he was trained, and may face an open-ended teaching and learning situation where courage, trust, imagination, creativity, and cooperation are essential attitudes and skills.

Teachers face problems in most programmes. They often know little about the community which is such an important part of the LBP curriculum. It is hard even to start thinking about how to cope with such an unknown entity. Many teachers do not have particular skills in such areas as curriculum planning, problem solving and management, not to mention the kinds of skills expected from the students according to Leendert van den Bosch; namely technical-instrumental skills, communication skills, political skills, value skills, and change skills. The teacher soon realizes what the teachers in the Tvind schools in Denmark have realized, namely 'that the same pedagogical principles apply to both pupils and teachers. .' (Chapter Five).

Many teachers find that the new situation demands considerably more work in the planning stages. Usually it means more administrative work in general, and it is also hard to plan and manage many programmes. It is quite clear that many LBP-teachers need support from other teachers, heads, and students.

In some cases (e.g. the Netherlands, see Chapter 2) teacher-resistance has been observed. A general feeling of insecurity in times of declining enrolment, the fear of losing jobs, and possible loss of status have been reported. These, however, are rather more rare reactions.

It has been the experience of the authors that, as a general rule, teachers involved in LBP programmes are enthusiastic about them. This might be a natural consequence of their own involvement and participation. In spite of the hard work, they prefer to continue their efforts. In earlier reports we have observed this as an effect of the 'pioneer-role' in educational innovations. We believe it also illustrates the importance of joint student and teacher ownership of projects.

The school as an organization

LBP programmes have important implications for the individuals involved. However, the consequences for the curriculum and the school as an organization might even be more fundamental. This depends largely on the degree of LBP involvement. Some selective programmes might be organized by an individual teacher, and leave the rest of the school untouched. In some cases, other teachers might even not know about the programme. Most programmes, however, are not subject-based but problem-oriented with implications for several subjects. Cooperation among teachers becomes an important factor. So does support from the school leadership.

The more fundamental a programme becomes, the more comprehensive the implications for the school as a whole. It should raise questions regarding the nature of the teaching-learning process, the nature of knowledge itself, the way the school day is organized, the role of the school in the community, the role of teachers and students, the implications for examinations, the consequences for school leadership, and the implications for the allocation of resources. As LBP programmes become an integrated part of the school curriculum a fundamental change of schooling is inevitable. The important point, however, is that a school might be able to choose the degree of its own commitment, and does not necessarily have to commit itself to comprehensive change.

It often seems very difficult to change in a systematic way. The power of the disciplines is one factor already noted. The bureaucracy of school is another element. Many secondary schools are large complexes dominated by rigid regulations and control mechanisms, and flexibility is not a very welcomed norm. But maybe a stronger controlling factor than any other is the examination system, in particular as implemented in the European context (e.g., Scandinavia, see Chapter Five).

The school system

The nations studied in this volume differ to a significant degree in terms of centralization. Norway and Holland have generally centralized systems, the UK and the US a high degree of local autonomy. In spite of this fact, however, we believe that many system implications are the same. We have noted the tendencies of almost any system to 'solve' the unemployment crisis through alternative programmes. In some cases schools might be mandated to implement certain programmes, in other cases strong 'transferable' programmes are disseminated, and in yet others resources are allocated to a certain type of programme. Since schools are not autonomous – and since most resources for innovative programmes are controlled centrally – all systems will be inclined to adapt (or co-opt) regardless of the degree of (formal) centralization.

The system has a regulating effect through the examination system as noted above. The selection and preparation of teachers is another important factor for an innovation that demands new attitudes, knowledge and skills. Maybe the most important barrier in the Scandinavian context is its *success* in providing equality of opportuity in the educational sector. Standardization of schooling has become a key strategy to equalize opportunities between the cities and the rural areas, between girls and boys, among socio-economic classes, and increasingly between generations. What is not fully understood, however, is that equal *access* might be provided through standardization, while equality in *outcomes* can only be achieved through variety, taking a number of student-school-community resources into account.

There is another important factor in most centralized systems. Teachers are used to being told what to do. It might be that recruitment to the profession reflects such expectations, and that a

completely new role where initiative and creativity are both crucial
might be difficult for many. Teachers so far involved have been
motivated and quite successful – but are they representative? We
believe that they are. Teachers in our view are no different from any
other professionals given the chance actively to participate in the
development of their own work situation. We believe that trust and
responsibility will release energies so far not fully utilized, and that
therefore job satisfaction will increase, which again will mobilize
further energies for the necessary changes involved.

The communities

How do local communities react to LBP programmes? So far the
reports are mainly positive, despite some unease at 'having the
students loose' in the community all day. More important, maybe,
are the reactions from the workplaces. Some unions are afraid of
cheap labour. Employers are afraid of additional costs and demand
payment for the 'interns'.

In the most successful cases the programmes become a task for
the entire community. Adults other than teachers are involved as
resource-persons, the community becomes the classroom, and we
think that students begin to see themselves as valuable resources for
the community. So far our reports indicate that only a few
programmes have progressed so far. Many projects are moving in
this direction, however, and the consequences are that the
community is also involved in the planning and implementation of
LBP programmes.

Learning by Participation – barriers to implementation

It is very difficult to deal with barriers to the implementation of any
reform because they pertain to the student, teacher, school, school
system, and the community levels and spread across value, power,
practical, and psychological issues. Since each of these barrier
dimensions can be analysed at any of the above-mentioned levels of
the school system we could, in theory, treat this section according to
a complex matrix where levels of the school system were matched
against types of barriers. Our data, however, is of a general nature

and we find such a rigid treatment less helpful that a more global one. We shall continue to look broadly at the various barriers that have been illustrated in this volume.

Value barriers

These are barriers that exist because individuals and groups have different ideologies and basic beliefs that make changes look quite different, depending on the perspective of the observer. Leendert van den Bosch in his discussions has called these barriers 'resistance' (see Chapter Two). Some teachers who reject present society, for example, would resist attempts to build bridges between the school and the community. Although there might still be some who believe that young people should be protected from society – and kept safely in schools – these values are rare. More important, maybe, are the arguments against LBP from discipline-oriented teachers who see LBP as a threat to a systematic subject-oriented curriculum, although many would contend that such arguments are basically a defence mechanism. Without doubt, some teachers have very basic difficulties with a problem-oriented approach to learning, since in their view it undermines the basic organization of knowledge as they see it.

Educators who have fought a hard battle for equality of educational opportunity and who see equality as nearly identical with standardization have a number of problems – on ideological grounds – with LBP. Is it not a danger that it will only be a programme for the drop-outs? Is it not simply a clever mechanism for separating out those who are less academically able?

Students so far see status as being mainly attached to academic disciplines. LBP programmes might be resisted simply because their 'qualities' are not appreciated.

Power barriers

These are barriers resulting from power redistribution in the system, which is often the result of significant innovations. We have already seen that the subject-based interest groups might well resist LBP programmes. In some cases teacher unions have felt that the role of

the teacher is undermined – both because his traditional information
-giving role is less vital, and because adults other than teachers
become resource persons. Individuals and groups outside the school
react in similar ways. Examination bodies will have less control,
unions might be afraid of 'cheap labour', local industry might be
afraid of competition, and the educational hierarchy will have more
difficulties managing the system. More basic, however, is the fact
that the student in LBP makes more decisions about his own
learning situation. In effect, LBP is real decentralization, a process
that in the long run will raise questions regarding the role and power
of educational bureaucracy.

Practical barriers

Sometimes innovations fail because they are badly conceived.
Resistance to adopting them is a natural reaction. At other times
barriers result from inadequate management of the innovation
process, resulting in unwanted practical problems for individuals
and groups. For many, LBP is not concrete enough. It is not a
defined programme but only some principles or ideas. They cannot
cope with the ambiguous situation and the uncertainties that
naturally lie ahead. The concept might even be looked upon as too
complex, too ambitious, and too idealistic for practical life.
Combined with this notion of complexity and idealism is often heard
the idea that only very motivated and particularly skilled teachers
will embark upon LBP programmes. Reactions are also coming from
students who might be afraid of losing credits and who are uncertain
of the consequences.

It is a fact that many LBP programmes pose new challenges for the
teacher or the school in planning and implementing the programmes.
It raises new kinds of problems and demands new skills and new
roles, often with very little preparation. Quite often the usual
support service does not help much, curriculum materials do not
exist, and those responsible – teachers, heads and students – are
embarking upon an open-ended learning situation.

School administrators have practical problems of a very real
nature. Large secondary schools, for example, have very little
flexibility in their organization (as they are now managed). LBP
programmes on a wide scale might introduce difficult problems. In

addition LBP introduces activities that traditional evaluation methods cannot cope with. In other words, how can anyone other than the student and the teacher know what is really happening?

There are practical problems in the environment as well. In some cases it has simply been difficult to find a sufficient number of practical, useful experiences. It takes considerable time and some creative work to develop concrete and valuable options. There are also some fears that although LBP might be quite successful on a small scale it will create fundamental problems if implemented on a large scale in any given community.

Psychological barriers

Sometimes individuals resist change in spite of the fact that the innovation does not challenge their values seriously or upset their power. There may not even be major practical problems connected with the innovation. At this stage we do not have data to indicate to what extent such psychological barriers are connected with LBP programmes. We do believe, however, that since LBP so often brings both students and teachers into the unknown, facing open-ended learning situations, many teachers (and students) might well be afraid even of trying it.

Strategies for Learning by Participation

Although there are major forces supporting LBP in society as well as in our schools, nothing is more important than the fact, simply, that most students and teachers are enthusiastic about LBP. Such enthusiasm is reported from all the countries studied in this volume. In a country like Holland, for example, there is now a general climate in favour of LBP, a conceptual framework is developed, local initiatives are centrally supported, resources are available, and LBP is not seen as a threatening force. The very fact that LBP is *not* a ready made programme is looked upon as a major strength. We would certainly agree that it is, and most studies on the implementation of educational innovations would confirm it; however, a local capacity for adaptations and development must exist.

We would also note a fundamental element in LBP that might be one of the most important and lasting factors. Skindro says: '. . pupils and teachers start out together in an open situation, in which they can and must make decisions themselves. .' (Chapter Five). The fact that the focus of control is moved down to the student—teacher level is quite fundamental.

For a long time teachers and our societies have been under pressure from forces that have limited their power, prestige, and opportunities. We see LBP as bringing the teacher back to a responsible role, together with his or her students. This might have more to do with job satisfaction and thereby with the success of LBP than any other single factor. We will now turn to some of the more promising strategies for the introduction of LBP programmes.

At the individual level

The teacher and the student need support of two kinds: 'shelter-conditions' that would protect them from 'punishment'; that is, the understanding of persons in authority that open-ended learning situations like LBP cannot be planned in the traditional way, that risks are involved and that the risks are worth taking. Secondly, they need technical support. The teacher needs to have access to the community, to get help in identifying community resources, to get to know other teachers with similar experiences, and get support from the school to develop necessary materials. Teachers do need some training as well, but the training on the job with the necessary support from other teachers and the students may be the most effective 'training' she or he can get.

At the school level

LBP poses problems for the school as an organization, both internally and in its relationship to the community. The school needs to build a problem-solving capacity internally, to cope with questions of curriculum organization, timetable, team-teaching, materials development, and evaluation. First, school management needs to be involved to create a minimum of individual teacher support – and if possible a general climate for LBP – within the school and the community. It is important to note that although a headmaster might support LBP, in no way does LBP need to be mandatory for all teachers. After all, LBP is often dependent on the creativity of the individual teacher and it is better to initiate a limited experiment that might grow slowly, than to mandate a change that has no chance of success; this might equally apply to the *nature* of the programmes. It might be wise to start out with an approach that has greater pedagogic respectability, and is less threatening to institutional establishments. It might be necessary to undertake a very careful assessment of attitudes within the staff, motivation of individual teachers, possibilities for school support and available resources in the community, in addition to the very basic process of assessing student needs for LBP.

At the community level

Community support is vital for LBP. Schools, in Europe at least, have isolated themselves from the community for such a long time that the notion of a closer integration might be overwhelming. It becomes vital, then, to interact frequently with individuals and groups in the community who might be interested in cooperative programmes. Since real cooperation is needed, these individuals and institutions should be brought into the decision-making process and thereby actively participate in the development of programmes.

Trying programmes that are less threatening, not competing with local jobs, may be recommended, or finding socially-useful programmes that are looked upon as being of real help. We believe that this approach would create a positive climate for LBP. Since LBP will be unknown to most parents as a programme option, great care should be taken to introduce them, as well as the community at large, to the potentials involved in the concept; it would be disheartening if the fears mentioned in earlier sections, that LBP becomes associated with 'drop-out' and 'failure' programmes, should be nurtured. Indeed, we believe that the way in which LBP is introduced is a vital factor affecting its future development.

At the system level

We maintain that LBP is not a programme but a set of principles to be applied to local learning situations. Although there are examples of centrally-developed programmes (e.g., Experienced Based Career Education in the USA) Dollar observes that the most successful EBCE-programmes are those that have been adapted to fit local situations (Chapter Four). We do not generally see a role for central Government in the development of ready made LBP-packages. But we do see a role for central authorities:

1. *Networking*: We believe that most innovations spread through personal contacts. Innovations travel not on paper, but with people. One of the most important strategies for central authorities would simply be to *stimulate* a process of renewal by bringing together experienced individuals (students, teachers, community members) to exchange experiences. In this process concrete help like the exchange of material is a natural part of the process. Let us again remind ourselves that the purpose is *not* to sell a particular programme but rather to initiate a process of innovation.

2. *Demonstration*: Although this could be conceived as a part of networking it might be seen as a separate activity. In a new field like LBP it might be quite useful simply to see a programme in operation. Some LBP projects are complex, and the best method of presenting them is to demonstrate their value. Central authorities in cooperation with local districts might encourage the development of 'demonstration-projects' to illustrate the wide range of options available to new practitioners.

3. *Evaluation*: In any new programme the knowledge base is weak. An ongoing programme of research and evaluation should be initiated by central authorities it being unlikely that local authorities would have the capacity to undertake them and, furthermore, quite useful material could be developed and used in local programmes.

4. *System modifications*: LBP might have implications for school laws, examinations' resource allocations, teacher-education, support-structures, and incentives. As LBP becomes an important and integrated part of school activities these questions need to be studied and necessary changes implemented. In an experimental phase, however, only 'shelter conditions' for experimentation might be necessary prior to any major modifications of the organization.

Outside the formal school system

In some countries the school is too rigid to undertake LBP programmes. Examples taken from this volume indicate that the informal system might well be better suited to initiate programmes of this nature. In the UK, Further Education establishments have often shown great flexibility in terms of curriculum alternatives. In the UK, the Department of Labour and volunteer organizations have shown interest and the ability to sponsor LBP activities. This is true for Scandinavia as well, where an organization like the Folks University – a non-formal institution – has developed radical LBP programmes.

LBP does respond to real needs, and organizations within or outside the formal school system may be used. We believe, however, that the most important mechanism for a more radical change in learning opportunities for our youth is the school. To modify our schools, then, to meet their needs more adequately, becomes a vital concern.

The future of Learning by Participation

Piet Hein, the Danish poet, has said: . .'there is nothing more difficult to predict than the future..' We do not attempt to predict the future of LBP, but we do believe it is important to look at some forces that might affect the chances for LBP implementation. The problem, of course, is that we can only assume that a given trend might continue – the art of extrapolation, in other words. We can say nothing about the consequences of new events. Having lived through the 70s, and looking back at the 'future scenarios' developed for this decade in the 60s, we cannot help but feel humble. Who could have predicted the oil crisis in 1973? Who would ever have dreamt of the unemployment situation at the end of this decade, partly as a consequence of the oil embargo? And the consequences for schools? We should, however, like to indicate some possibilities that might alter the future of LBP significantly.

New technology:

The introduction of micro-processors is a case in point. Present predictions indicate that nearly half of all office clerical jobs will be gone by 1990, and similar trends are envisaged in other fields as well. What will it do to schooling? Will LBP be seen as another threat to job security? Will jobs be even more computerized and specialized, and what will that do to the possibilities for youth participation?

New job expectations:

Are we heading towards a society where a large portion of the adult population will never have a job? Is it possible that not only a small minority of 'underachievers' but also a large group of motivated young people will never be able to practise in a job that 'pays off'? If that is the case, what does it mean to human motivation, self respect, family life, and the upbringing of children? In our view the only possibility is to create new types of jobs, not associated with the production of goods, but seen rather as new types of opportunities in the human service sector. In other words, this would mean that many of the unpaid jobs in our communities today – often associated with leisure activities – would be looked upon as being important and socially useful, and would be well paid. Of course, it might mean that LBP programmes would be looked upon as very appropriate vocational preparation programmes, but it could also mean that there would be fewer areas where young people could work without threatening the jobs of adults.

More important may be that the definition of what work actually is – and what education and leisure are – might be challenged in the not too distant future, as we have already discussed.

New social expectations:

Our expectations are rapidly changing. The social welfare state, in particular in Scandinavia, has already had an important impact upon our attitudes toward life. The traditional competitive values of capitalistic societies are not as apparent as before. Social security and a heavy tax system has created new conditions for careers and for family life. Industrial democratization has created new expectations toward the job.

Already, changing social expectations have an important impact on schooling. Young people have other career goals than before – or at least, it is not certain that a given trend in terms of career expectations will continue. Our societies are searching for a new life style in post-industrial society with an increasingly international reality at our doorstep. It will have an unpredictable impact on concepts like LBP, which are searching for new approaches to learning.

The lesser developed world:

Compared with the problems of young people in the less-developed nations, ours are very small. Partly as a consequence of the gradual development of these nations, our life styles will have to change. The world in which our children will live is certainly going to look different from the one we thought we had developed. One of the most important forces shaping the future will be the increasingly important position of developing nations in the world picture.

What does this have to do with schools and LBP? We believe it could have a dramatic effect. Firstly it will mean that school curricula will have to change. Students must be much better prepared to live in an increasingly complex world – and to have at least some knowledge about other nations as well as the skills to deal with the challenges ahead is a fundamental necessity. We also see a possibility for more active exchange of young people among nations, in particular between industrialized nations and the less-developed countries. Why could not LBP programmes be organized abroad? Why cannot the young people of other nations work cooperatively in our schools? These ideas might sound rather 'far out', but might be closer to realization than we think.

Schools as monopolies of knowledge:

Will the trend towards challenging the position of the school as a monopoly of knowledge continue? The last decade has shown the importance of the mass media, the strength of non-formal education, and the importance of recurrent education and on-the-job training. The school is no longer the sole institution of providing knowledge to the next generation. Assuming that the trend continues, what does it mean to the very existence of schooling as we know it today?

And what would it mean to LBP?

We believe that LBP is the answer. Schools can no longer assume a knowledge-dissemination role in isolation from the community. Young people will no longer accept a life here and now that is not useful and meaningful for themselves and for society. Knowledge will be defined less and less in terms of subject structures, and will be seen increasingly as problem-oriented and integrated with critical-theoretical reflection. In our view, schools will continue to exist as institutions that can 'bring the complex world together' by helping people to explore themselves and the world in which they live.

IMTEC was established by the OECD Centre for Educational Research and Innovation as a management training and development project. Since January 1977, it has been a totally independent, non-profitmaking educational foundation under Norwegian law, operating from its current base in Oslo. Enquiries and further contact should be directed to the Oslo address as follows:

IMTEC
Rosenhof Skole
Dynekil Gata 10
OSLO 5
Norway.